Jill, Hospice Nurse
Book 2
Last Exit

Michal Poe

Copyright © 2012 Michal Poe
All rights reserved.

ISBN: 1-4791-2889-9
ISBN-13: 9781479128891

Love doesn't stop with death

MONDAY

It was a little damp out, as some dew was still on the grass, so as Jill approached the grave, her shoes were getting wet. She'd had to ignore the No Trespassing sign, and she thought it ironic that next to that was a sign that said No Digging. She'd driven four miles out of her way to stop by her patient, Manny's, final resting place, and she was not to be deterred. He'd been a homeless wanderer for most of his short life. His last residence was in a doghouse he'd found behind the fire station. His whole family was a little strange. He came from a line of pioneer gold miners up in the hills who had stuck it rich more than one hundred years earlier. Most of them became reclusive.

Behind a small grove of trees was Manny's family's graveyard, something not seen too often. Manny had been stitched up in a canvas bag and laid in a deep hole, right next to his grandparents. His mother had said there was no headstone yet, but Jill could tell where the grave was because it had sunk in some and needed more soil on top. That sort of thing didn't happen with professional gravediggers. She was shocked when she saw an obvious temporary headstone made out of wood. It had letters in white paint that said, "I, Emmanuel am long gone, dead. Don't put a shovel in my head." She didn't know whether Manny had arranged to have that epithet and his parents had sanctioned it or if it was a prank. She came close to yanking it out, but then

Michal Poe

she realized it was none of her business and she needed to let things be. She did say a short prayer, since Manny had asked her to do that, and a promise was a promise. Then she headed back to her Jeep.

In her small foothill community, most everyone knew everyone. And Jill Wheaten, a long-time hospice nurse, knew more than most about how people lived their lives. Every family is touched by death at one point or another. Jill lived in a more rural area, up the hill. There she had some acreage for her beloved avocation, organic vegetable farming.

The only place she was not familiar with was the suburban sprawl of newly built beautiful homes along River Road. Though she admired the architecture, as she drove to see her official first patient, by the name of Robert Goulden, she couldn't take the time to enjoy sightseeing. Hospice nurses were now scheduled to see six patients throughout the day, so she hoped she could knock out this assignment in a hurry. Her quick stop at Manny's graveside had been on her own time.

Mr. Goulden had applied for hospice care a week after his reported death. There was much confusion over this man's legitimacy. It was now up to Jill, the most experienced nurse at Community Hospice, to determine if this new patient, recently released from the hospital, was in fact the real man—the Goulden who'd faithfully paid his medical insurance premiums for the past thirty years. Or was he, as the hospice director suspected, a usurper.

Apparently, Robert Goulden had been in amazingly good health until he dropped dead at the poker table at his regular hangout, Pansy's Card Room. The coroner on call had resisted the urge to write, in his official report, *The dead man was found still clutching his royal flush.* It wouldn't be the first heart attack on record due to that hand. The medical examiner surmised that this flush was the real dead man's hand, as it certainly was more lethal than aces and eights.

Having arrived at the proper address without much of a plan as to how to go about her sleuthing assignment, Jill gamely gathered her nursing bags and paperwork from her vehicle. She admired the lovely array of English garden flowers along the formal walkway. Although she had slowed her life down, she still never took the time to actually smell the roses. But at least this morning she could breathe in their sweet aromas as she rang the chiming doorbell of the grand Tudor house. A stately looking elderly man answered the door. She half expected to be addressed as Madame.

Mr. Goulden was dressed in a smoking jacket. At least that's what Jill assumed it was. Either that or a very ugly, plaid sport coat. She could imagine him as a handsome and distinguished-looking man in his younger days. Now, he appeared cautious, wise, and old—certainly older than his stated age of sixty-one. He walked with great care as he slowly ushered Jill into the wood-paneled library.

"Osteoporosis," he stated, after he'd probably noticed Jill's estimate of his gait. "Side effect of the recent treatments."

Jill, dressed in colorful, loose scrubs, felt underdressed. She was glad her shoes had dried somewhat. She gingerly sat in a wing chair. Very cautiously, so as not to disturb the various objets d'art on a side table next to the chair, she spread out her paperwork.

When Goulden settled into his chair, she began her normal questioning. With due care, she wrote down all his answers. The questions covered his personal data, family history, and onset of disease, as well as his current medications, drug and alcohol consumption, sleep, exercise, and bowel and eating habits. She also asked about his religious and fraternal affiliations, mental outlook, and coping patterns. Finally, Jill asked what he hoped hospice services could provide for him since, officially, he had less than six months to live. Mr. Goulden's replies were given in a quiet, contemplative manner.

"Quite thorough you are, my dear," he commented well into the interview.

If only you knew, Jill thought. Knowing Bill Bracken, her supervisor, she had even suspected he might want everything voice recorded, so she'd carefully checked her nursing bag before leaving the office that morning, half expecting to find a wire.

Toward the end of the interview, there was a tap at the library door. Hearing it, Mr. Goulden politely asked Jill, "Ms. Wheaten, do you mind if I have my tea now? My staff usually brings it to me promptly at nine-thirty."

Jill nodded her consent.

"It would please me greatly to have you join me."

Jill nodded again.

"Enter," Mr. Goulden said in a slightly raised voice, as he looked toward the doorway.

The door opened. A young woman in a formal, black and white uniform pushed a cart into the room. Mr. Goulden politely introduced Charise, the maid, as she served.

"One lump or two?" she asked Jill.

"Two, thank you."

Jill used the distraction of the tea setup to pull a scrunchie out of the pocket of her scrubs and contain her usually unruly, curly hair into a somewhat proper-looking bun. She was actually hungry, having not had time for breakfast or even any office snacks.

She'd been briefed on this assignment right after this Monday's morning team meeting. Her boss had admonished her, "Just go out there. Delve into, in a very low-key way, this man's life. Compare your physical findings to the few facts the medical reviewers were able to obtain from the health records of the authentic man."

Jill wasn't new to her profession; she'd held the same nursing job for the past ten years. During that time she'd more than once harbored a few suspicions over whether certain patients were truly who and what they said they were. Medical insurance fraud wasn't something new either, but it seemed to be more prevalent in recent years. It made Jill sad that a man would have to steal someone's medical card to get health care—specifically, and more to the point, end of life care. What had the medical field and hospice nursing come to? How could the nurses be expected to do the policing, when all they wanted to do was care for people? Logical deduction was a natural gift Jill possessed. That, along with her years of experience, was probably the reason she'd been given this patient. But she liked to use her skills for people's benefit, not for their detriment.

Jill really enjoyed being feted with a lovely cup of tea and toast points. She felt as if she'd fallen into an English play. Whether it was a drama or a comedy, though, she couldn't yet tell.

Michal Poe

As the dishes were cleared away, she noticed a slight odor and figured Goulden apparently preferred a little brandy in his morning tea. To be fair, he'd admitted during the data-gathering—citing social necessity—his habit of consuming one or two alcoholic drinks per day. However, Jill made a mental note, deducing that starting this early in the morning wasn't exactly a healthy sign.

After tea, she washed up, laid out her necessary equipment, and accomplished the physical exam. With a little brandy in him, Mr. Goulden became more talkative.

"Wonderful," Mr. Goulden told her, "I don't think I've ever had as good a physical, even at my doctor's office."

Ordinarily, Jill would have been flattered, but now she felt a little guilty. She kept looking at the notes from her supervisor as to what she should be looking for. She'd found the gall bladder removal scar, but many people had that operation, and the scar was usually in the same place.

"I had that cholestectomy about five years ago from Dr. Amay," Mr. Goulden offered. "I remember, I told that doctor, 'Without my bile my wit has no bite.'"

Goulden must have thought that comment was top rate because it got the first smile out of him. Jill smiled too, but hers was forced. She just didn't get that type of English humor.

Again referring to her notes, she saw that she was to check for a large mole, which she hoped she would find in order to care for this patient. She looked, and found no mole. She commented upon his unusually clear skin.

"Had all my moles burned off, especially the big one near the right buttock. Dr. Amay recommended a wonderful dermatologist. He used a marvelous, new laser technology," the apparently real Robert Goulden said.

"Ahh," Jill exhaled, greatly relieved.

Now simply curious and wondering if there was anything she'd missed, Jill ventured to say, "You know your name is very familiar. I think I read something in the paper about a man named Robert Goulden. It couldn't have been you, though, because he apparently died quite suddenly."

Mr. Goulden's face fell. He choked out his words. "No… Robert Goulden? Here…in this city? Died you say…when?"

Jill had no choice but to go on, "Yes. Last week. Died suddenly." Jill repeated. Noting his distress, she added, "I'm sorry."

Goulden covered his face with his hands as he slumped down in his chair. Then suddenly he lowly lamented, "Oh, no. My father? He was my daddy…"

Now truly alarmed, Jill stood and walked over to the side of his chair. Coming from this patient, those words sounded so unexpected. She reached down and put her hand on his shoulder as a display of support and waited. She waited quite a while as he sobbed. When he had calmed somewhat, she went back to her chair and waited some more.

That's how she heard his story. In the long run, it was no more unusual than many. Jill had listened to so many stories through the years. The things that are really important in life came to people's attention when time was short. Their memories made them cry or laugh, or simply provoked poignant smiles. He told of his long quest to find his father. And, how when he had, his father wanted nothing to do with him.

Goulden sighed, and now looked directly at Jill. "I've made a lot of money. My son is capable of making his own millions, but still, I had to make up a legacy for myself. I kept the hope I could see him again. I would have last month, except for all this medical testing." His eyes were teary again as he continued, "This one part of my own life, which will soon come to an end, will remain undone," he ended with dramatic intonation.

Jill sat quietly with him. You can't hurry through deep emotions, and Jill had no intention of doing so in this case. She waited, and when he began to stir in his chair, she handed him more tissues and then quietly began to pack up her workbags.

When he spoke again, he was calm. "Thank you for listening," he said. "I don't think I've ever told anyone my whole story before."

"You've had quite a shock today, Mr. Goulden. You're an amazing person to have loved your father so much all through these years." Then she took a chance, as she did from time to time, and added, slowly and compassionately, "Love doesn't stop with death."

Goulden looked at her for a long moment, nodded, and took another long moment. Then he said, in his more normal and very formal voice, "Thank you, and please call me Robert."

***

Thus Jill began her usual appointed rounds for the day. She carefully repacked her bag and made her way back down the lovely flowered path to her Jeep. She checked the address of her next patient. With five more visits to make, she had no time to waste.

She'd driven these same low foothills for many, many years. She knew shortcuts that weren't even on the map.

Burnhills was more than three thousand feet above sea level, so even with the normal hot weather down in the valley her community had four seasons. It made it a lovely place to live, but it meant she had to drive in all kinds of weather. Today was a wonderfully cool summer morning. Once she got on the main road, she rolled down her window to get a little fresh air. Then she reached over and turned off her GPS. The voice would only distract her from her own thoughts.

Driving past the home of the Kalleens, one of whom was a former patient, Jill remembered that they had also had some sort of identity theft problem. Alan was his name, and he was such a joy to have in the program. Jill felt lucky to have been assigned the case. It seemed Alan's wallet had been stolen and he'd commented it didn't make any difference at this point. Sure enough, his wife Margery reported, they'd gotten big credit card bills and calls from collection agencies. She'd remarked that the thieves were traveling everywhere she'd wanted to go.

The final straw was Alan's arrest warrant for overdue child support payments for three young children living in Louisiana! The claim was ridiculous, since the Kalleens were childless, but Margery also told Jill she'd begun to harbor an irrational belief. She'd started thinking that if the thieves stole Alan's name, then they had to steal his illness too. She'd told Jill that if he had to be considered a deadbeat father or even go to jail for life, at least she'd be able to visit him there.

Michelle Grant, the hospice social worker, said this was a simple case of working through difficult transitions. Jill thought there should be a harder phrase for such emotional pain.

Michal Poe

Alan had died over a year ago. Jill still saw Margery from time to time, coming to or going from the hospice bereavement support classes for widows.

Now, a traffic detour sent her the long way around to get back downtown. Turning off that GPS might not have been so wise after all. Jill shifted in her seat and slipped off her white clogs, which she noted had a little green staining around the soles. She sipped some hot tea from her thermos, kept in her console. Trying to relax as she drove, she now had time to reflect on all that had transpired earlier in the morning, before she'd set out to see Goulden. There had been added pressure during the team meeting at the hospice office. The first order of business had been the fact that the team was outgrowing its space.

"Team, you are not to be concerned, but management will begin to look for new office options since our lease will be up soon." Bill had announced.

That news was both good and bad. It was good because everyone had felt the space pinch for some time, and bad because it was always hard to adjust to a move.

Aside from the possible move, the manager had announced that tomorrow he would go over a new, mandated patient count process he was implementing. This would be interesting to hear. They had tried many such "accountability" schemes before, but Bill Bracken was a little more aggressive than most managers. Admittedly, she and her co-workers were a little anxious. They wondered what scheme this man, who had no idea of the complications and stresses involved in their everyday job, would propose on Tuesday.

***

Amazingly, even with the detour, Jill wasn't too far behind schedule when she arrived at her next patient's home. Janice Stearn had emphysema. She'd been struggling with the end stages of her disease for over a year. Jill had been making weekly visits for all that time.

After Jill made her way through the unlocked front door, which the patient had left propped open, she noticed things were becoming more disorderly in the home. Janice's home office was spilling over into the kitchen area. As slim as Jill was, she still had to maneuver carefully in order to get to the sink to wash up before beginning her routine assessment and checking vital signs.

Janice was still able to run her business, Angels/Angles. It was a small business financial backing group—a difficult business in hard economic times, but she appeared to do well. And she did it all from her dining room table, since she could no longer get out and about.

Jill was surprised this patient functioned at all, because she was indeed very weak. Her arms looked like small sticks, and her skin was paper thin and bruised easily because of the poor circulation. In most cases this advanced, Jill would have found the patient bed bound, but Janice really pushed herself. Jill had never seen anyone at this stage of the illness—with practically no breath sounds, using pursed lip breathing, and having oxygen levels turned up to maximum level allowed for her illness—accomplish the prodigious amount of work Janice was still able to conduct.

Jill could barely get a word in edgewise with all the interruptions of urgent e-mails, phone calls, texts, and faxes. Janice even had a beeper, which would go off from time to time. Jill did manage to get the information she needed, but it took a while. Toward the end of her visit, Jill noticed, on top of one stack of paperwork, a one-way ticket to Baltimore. Janice's name was printed on it, clear as a bell. Jill needed to talk to her about that.

"Janice," Jill said, "I need just a few minutes of your undivided attention."

Janice looked up in a distracted way. She sighed, turned off several of her gadgets, and faced Jill. "Five minutes of undivided attention," she forced out, all in one breath.

"I appreciate that, very much. Janice, I don't usually interfere at all with what patients wish to do. You've accomplished so much. But what I'm worried about is travel. With your condition, and even with the extra expense of obtaining oxygen on the flight, an airplane ride would be too exhausting at this stage of your illness. Your business…"

Here, Janice interrupted her and, breathing strenuously between sentences, admonished Jill. "Is my business. But you *are* observant not to mention snoopy."

Jill kept quiet as she could tell Janice seemed to want to add more.

"If you worked in my field, you'd be getting better money."

"Janice," Jill cautioned, although she couldn't hide a slight smile after Janice's last sentence, "We need to go back to the subject at hand. I know your doctors wouldn't approve of this travel. Will you please reconsider?"

"No. Absolutely no." Now scowling, Janice crossed her arms and asked, "Is our little talk over?"

"I was promised five minutes Janice. Just now, I couldn't even register a blood pressure. I don't know what you're running on."

"Time lost. Opportunities missed. And, I'm going to Baltimore!"

Jill didn't get to use any more of Janice's time as she turned her back on Jill and restarted all her machines. Jill packed up her things and quietly did her reports while Janice continued her business affairs. Apparently Janice was running on the fuel of regret.

Jill paused before she left the home and gave Janice a big hug. Jill wasn't surprised that Janice readily accepted that gesture.

"You're amazing." Jill said.

Janice replied, "I only wish I'd known that sooner in my life."

Striding back to her Jeep and reloading her nurse's bag, Jill thought about Janice's line, "Lost time, opportunities missed." It brought to mind regrets over how her marriage had ended. Once in a while, it still haunted her.

The breakup between her and Chris had been acrimonious. He'd had no idea that Jill wasn't going to continue to support him financially and emotionally his whole life. She'd tried so hard, too hard, to make his life the way he wanted it. Or perhaps it was the way she wanted it for him. The more she grew spiritually, emotionally, and mentally, the weaker he became. She gained self-confidence from her nursing career and felt she was finding her true place in life. When she had her son, it was wonderful; she felt it completed her. But Chris thought he was being replaced. They were unbalanced.

She had finally lost respect for him when she realized that not only was he trying to blame her for all that didn't go right with him, but he stopped any physical closeness because he said she emasculated him. The funny thing was, he might have been right.

Jill didn't ask, and he didn't pay child support. Another mistake, she'd later realized. A financial investment in their son might have helped him stay more involved in Jason's life. He'd remarried and he lived in another state and had two little girls. He'd only seen Jason twice in the past ten years. And both visits were very brief.

For years, she'd lived with these misgivings. It wasn't until her mother became ill with dementia and her son became more independent that she realized these regrets were keeping her from looking at her own future. All along, she kept thinking the hard part would be forgiving Chris; it turned out it was much more important for her to forgive herself.

It was only a while ago; she'd allowed herself to begin dating again. Her boyfriend, Bennett, was a first baby step toward healing.

***

Jill drove up to her third morning patient's home. She stretched her legs when she got out of her Jeep and went to the hatch to pluck out what she'd need for the visit. She was squeezing Dan Coultran in because his home was close, and then she'd still have time to go by the office around lunchtime to pick up the oxygen meter for an afternoon patient. She'd wished she'd had it along to check Janice. There weren't enough meters for each nurse. The budget wouldn't allow for that, she was told. But next year everyone would be assigned one, Bill had assured the staff. Jill had purchased a few of her own items, out of her own funds, but the O2 meter was too expensive and too easy to lose for Jill to subsidize. She'd have to wait for the blessed purchase order.

Mrs. Coultran, Stevie, answered the door and rather hurriedly escorted Jill into the study, where Dan was resting in an easy chair. He was seventy-three and always dressed nattily when Jill visited. Jill's entrance into the room seemed to awaken him from a short nap. He'd become sick very suddenly, and the reality of his terminal diagnosis was only beginning to set in for him. Jill had rightly predicted at the time of the initial sign up that he might take quite a while to work out his feelings. Jill knew he'd been seen by the on-call hospice nurse over the weekend, but just for a prescription refill. She planned to have a talk with him and his wife and help them get his medicines a little more organized. Then a precious weekend visit, which was normally reserved for more emergent problems, wouldn't have to be used for something as simple as running out of pills.

"Hello, Jill," he smiled. "I've been waiting for you."

"Glad to see you too," Jill greeted. She noted he looked very alert.

Stevie said nothing. She took a chair near a small desk in the corner. She looked extremely tired.

Jill washed up and proceeded with her checkup. Dan's health was about the same as it'd been at her last visit.

She was about to go over the medicine regimen when Stevie motioned behind Dan's back and silently hinted that she needed to talk to Jill. Jill excused herself for a moment, as she had to get some disease-specific literature from her Jeep anyway. Stevie followed her to the door.

"When you come back inside, Jill, tell Dan no more sex!"

"Umm…" Jill answered, "well, I can bring in some information about intimacy and illness for you to look over, when I get the other information for you. Would that help?"

"No, just tell him no nookie. He's killing me!"

"I'll be back with the literature. Then, if it's all right with you I'll bring up the subject in an open way and see if the two of you can come to some kind of compromise. Also," Jill suggested, "the social worker can come out."

Stevie glared at Jill.

Jill continued, "She comes out in many, many cases for clarification on issues. She works for the hospice and you can be assured Michelle is discreet and very professional."

Stevie had no comment. She continued to frown and stood standing at the open door waiting for Jill's return.

Jill had recently added a new bin to her already bulging Jeep's hatch. Aside from her nursing supplies, equipment, and personal things she needed on her job, she now included a smaller bin of appropriate printouts. She would leave some of these materials in the home at opportune times. The written literature included what to expect at one month, one week, one day, and even one hour before death. Also there were before death arrangement organizers, caregiver tips, ways to break the news to relatives and friends at various developmental stages, how to report changes in the patient's condition, who to call at time of death, and several general bereavement brochures. She didn't always give these handouts to everyone, but they were helpful for those who refused to see Michelle, the hospice social worker, or Kim, the chaplain, for spiritual counsel. On occasion she'd go over many of these topics herself, but the main reason for carrying the handouts was to prepare the way for Michelle.

Jill once joked that she was John the Baptist and that meant Michelle was…well as Michelle put it, "Yes, it's true, I go to the homes and give them the 'come to Jesus' talks!" Jill wasn't exactly sure what that meant, only that it usually worked and patients and staff were very appreciative of the social worker's help.

Jill pawed through her stash and found the right literature to bring back into the home.

Stevie met her there at the door and escorted her back into the sitting room, but on the way there she stated, "I don't think he has any idea this is to be his last exit!"

Intrigued by the term, since she hadn't heard it before, Jill asked, "What did your husband do for a living before he retired?"

She wasn't surprised when Stevie answered, "Big rig truck driving. He managed forty drivers."

Now settled in with the two of them sitting across from her, Jill broached the subject, as she'd promised Stevie.

"I meant to ask the two of you, in general, how are you doing these days?" Plowing on, she continued, "I know that illness can change the intimacy level, and that is very much a part of who patients are. Do you have any concerns in that area?"

"No. None for me," Dan beamed. "It couldn't be better. With that little blue pill, things are booming."

"Oh you're taking something for erectile dysfunction. I see," Jill said. Turning to Stevie, she said, "And, Stevie, how do you feel about this?"

Stevie, obviously not wanting to speak on the subject but hoping Jill would miraculously resolve her concerns in her favor, said nothing.

Michal Poe

"She's doing fine with it, huh, Honey? Just like the old honeymoon days," Dan barked.

This was too much, even for Stevie. She didn't answer her husband but looked at Jill. Speaking a little too loudly, with a shrill tone, she spewed, "I thought I was going to get a rest this weekend. I'm not as young as I used to be. However, when he ran out of his little blue pills, Dan got a nurse out here and a volunteer brought a whole new slew out on Saturday afternoon."

"So that was the reason for the weekend visit?"

"Yes," Dan interjected, totally ignoring his wife's tone. "Isn't that wonderful? The woman who brought it was a little embarrassed. You see, I said to her, 'I could take you all on!' I don't know. I was feeling so frisky. I didn't mean what it sounded like though. I apologized. I hope she didn't say anything to you about it."

Stevie raised her eyebrows and looked toward Jill, and her expression said it all. As in—didn't I tell you?

"Sometimes, a compromise is needed to find the right intimacy level for both partners." Jill ventured. "Dan, our social worker, Michelle, has great expertise in this area, and I'd like to send her out to explore this subject in a more detailed manner."

"Well, I don't know about that."

Stevie, recovering after her outburst and realizing her opportunity, said, "What a good idea." Turning to Dan, she added, "Let's do that soon, Honey. Think of how good it is for us to be getting so close again, after all these years."

Dan looked unconvinced but nodded his consent.

The visit was over, so Jill started for the door. Stevie followed her along the hallway as Jill was making her way out.

"See how he is? I told you so! I'm getting too old. I refuse to fake it. Enough is enough."

Jill could tell Stevie didn't really want an answer to those comments. She just needed a venting conduit. So Jill just said, "Uh-huh," as she left.

As she climbed into her vehicle, she was really happy that she'd finally made a successful exit from the home. She turned on her speakerphone and made a call to Michelle regarding the Coultrans' issues.

"Sure," Michelle said, "I can get to them tomorrow. Aside from the obvious lack of communication, I'll give them my Intimacy 101 instructions. If that doesn't work I'll go to the big guns."

"What are the big guns?" Jill asked. "Or can you even talk about it over the phone?"

"No, it's simple really. I've only had to use it a few times so far."

Jill's curiosity was really piqued. "Okay. And that is?"

"Well I have to finesse it, but the bottom line is this: I tell them that to get pleasure from an act in which the other person obtains nothing, even if seemingly consensual, could also be considered a sign of abuse."

"Wow. That's heavy. I'm afraid I may have to use it."

"Not with patients, Jill. It has to be presented in a very methodical way."

"No, not with patients," Jill said. "But with my boyfriend. Things aren't working out in that area."

"Okay, I wish I could say TMI, but it's not. Anyway, I know you'll end up telling me all about it!"

***

Michal Poe

Jill had to return to the office to pick up that oxygen meter, and returning to the office at mid-day could be a problem. There were many concerns that came up during the day, and the nurses could not always be reached immediately in the field. Sometimes they were in the middle of a procedure, and other times they just might have been out of range for the phones to ring through. So when Jill went back in the office, she knew she might be bombarded with some emergency or another. As she entered the low, gray, older building that Community Hospice leased, she surveyed the tight spaces. Oh, it was so true they needed more room. The staff was crammed into one small work area with only three partial partitions serving as cubicles along one wall.

One partition was for Donna Spreeze, volunteer coordinator and patient scheduler. She had to do interviews, data gathering, and also counsel the volunteers in a very tiny space.

Another cubicle was reserved for the physical therapist, Lurline Bridges. Filled with various pieces of equipment used for demonstration, the cubicle appeared rather draconian. Lurline used every usable inch of that cubicle. Aside from all the written materials she stored in there, the back brick wall was arrayed with hanging samples of canes, crutches, and braces. It was dangerous to try and walk in that area. Only Lurline, who was extremely athletic, could nimbly navigate the space.

The third was for the chaplain, Kimberly Clennons. Her cubicle was the smallest, but in fact she had begun to take over the storage area, which was crowded enough as it was. Kim, as she liked to be called, was the worst of the hoarders and continually brought in things she thought she just had to have. Most everyone else had given up on adding anything new. The rule was, if you brought something in, something had to go out.

Dean Cornell, the bereavement counselor, had a small, actual office in the opposite corner, where he did bereavement therapy with individuals or very small groups. Near that corner were partially obscured shelves where the patient records were stored. This was a very busy area at certain times of the day. A storeroom along another windowless wall held nursing supplies, equipment, and all kinds of necessary storage that any office serving ten or more people accumulates. Then right down the middle of that room were three tables pushed together with phones, computer monitors, paper supplies, and reference books. Four or five chairs were usually grouped around this space for the three nurses, the bathing aide, and the social worker. It was a tight fit. Therefore, many functions would overflow into the conference room connected to the space. That room had a refrigerator and also a restroom in the corner. The conference room was used for morning team meetings and education classes. It also served as a break room. A door on the far wall connected to a small anteroom from which there was a back entrance into Bill Bracken's office. Bill's office was a lovely space. The workers seldom entered there. It was by invite only, and it usually entailed some sort of infraction—or extra assignment.

There was a joke in home health/hospice circles that office accommodations were kept sparse to insure the workers would stay in the field rather than be tempted to come back to a comfortable space. This thinking sounded too manipulated to Jill, and she chose not to believe it.

Michal Poe

After she put her bag on top of her work area, she looked around the office to see who was still there. She only saw Donna, who was doing paperwork at her desk in the corner cubicle, and Dean, the bereavement counselor. Dressed in his usual black cotton turtleneck, he was sitting near two men. Jill recognized Richard, one of the oldest and most reliable volunteers. He was staring intently at someone who was sitting toe to toe with him. Both were sitting on straight-backed chairs, toward the back of the room. The guys' legs were in the open stance position. Jill remembered that move from her listening training class. She'd used it once or twice but found for nurses this stance could easily be misinterpreted. The volunteers didn't have their arms open and relaxed, though. In fact, they had them crossed and were staring daggers at each other. It was quiet in the room. To Jill, it looked a little unusual. That thought coming from a ten-year hospice nurse who'd seen it all meant something.

Dean made a shushing sound and walked over to her desk to explain.

Speaking quietly, he said, "Remember Richard and Stuart? When they both came in at about the same time this morning to see Donna regarding a volunteer project, they almost had a fight. It seems they knew each other in some previous employment, before Richard retired. There's some kind of old grudge."

"And the purpose of this is…?" Jill asked, also very quietly as well, as she motioned toward the two men.

"It's a new method of reconciliation I'm developing. This is the first trial. They have to sit across from each other for as long as it takes."

"As kids, my brother and I used to do that. We called that a stare down. Whoever blinked first, lost." Jill offered.

"Similar, but I certainly hope more sophisticated than that."

"What's the theory behind this?"

"The idea is to get the parties involved to sit it out, until one of them capitulates. You see," Dean continued, "the area, their distance apart, has to be precisely of a certain size. In a smaller fight arena, there are more ways a combatant can be injured, even inadvertently. Everything is compressed, physically and psychologically."

"You mean nowhere to run, or that you may get hit from something ricocheting?" Jill questioned, trying to understand.

"Yes, people don't realize, but there's a reason the boxing or wrestling rings have finalized into their exact dimensions. This collateral damage thing is a universal truth. That's why balance in life is important. Otherwise your emotional life gets too small. People begin to feel trapped and somebody either ends up getting hurt or curling up in a ball in the corner."

That hit a little close to home, Jill thought. That was exactly why she was so desperately seeking more balance in her own life.

Dean added, "Even though there's nothing going on physically, you see, in the psyche there's a lot going on."

"My, that's interesting," Jill stated, although she still wasn't exactly sure of all that Dean meant.

"And it's all taking place right here before our eyes," Dean added in his usual serious tone.

Jill thought about what he'd said for a while. Then Jill, ever practical, asked, "What about bathroom breaks?"

"Every two hours they get five minutes. Taking turns of course. We couldn't have them both in there at the same time. This has to be precisely coordinated. It's a true study of my new theory. Bill's expecting me to get a paper out of it. We'll see how it turns out. I didn't perceive it to be so tiring for me, though. They've both been in that same position for one hour. In fact, could you please watch them while I take a restroom break?"

"Sure, as long as my name is second on the paper," she teased. She went over to the other straight-backed chair and sat, thinking her own thoughts for a few minutes, until Dean returned with a grateful and relieved expression on his face.

"Thanks," he whispered.

Jill rearranged her nursing bag, picked up the oxygen meter, and then ate a quick lunch. Lately, she'd been pretty good about bringing something nutritious for herself. This was hard for her. She hadn't packed something for her son Jason since he'd started high school three years ago. Recently, she'd been relieved of the duty of leaving a lunch out on the counter for her mother. Weekdays she took her demented mom to the family adult day care home. They made lovely meals for her, and hand fed her too, if she was unable to manage the silverware.

Jill could rattle that title, *demented mother,* off her tongue now. She was more used to it. Initially, though, it was such a shock. She'd had to watch her robust mother, with such an interesting mind, go to pot, so to speak. Dementia. No known cause. No cure. She wanted to get her mother into a heredity study, but she wasn't sure if that was the best thing for her mom. She'd have to go through the blood tests and all. Also, Jill feared learning that she might experience the same fate as her mom. For her son, Jason, though, she knew it would be the responsible thing for her to do.

She had full custody of her mother and her affairs. Michelle had helped with that early on. The dementia center had told her that most people wait until it's too late and end up in court. That was sad. Yet she might have been one of those, except for the fact that she was reminded—nagged really—by the social worker and others to take action. She'd found a good lawyer, got all the things ready, and then, truth be known, had to use duplicity, some little deception, to talk her mom into going in and signing the papers.

That had been one of the hardest things Jill had ever had to do, but she'd done it. The staff in the lawyer's office didn't seem concerned that her mom was a little off the mark. Stina was much more alert than 90 percent of the cases they tried to help. Now it was official: Jill had full guardianship.

She was also trying to adjust to the fact that, come next summer, Jason would be in college. She didn't want to cling to him, but even with her mother in day care, it seemed the weekends were taken up with Stina's care, household errands, and her farm work. She and Jason didn't have much time to just sit and talk anymore. Carving out a little more time for family was on her to do list. Jill was really beginning to take steps in striving to expand her life these days, but she was not yet meeting her goal.

Just as she was ready to leave, Kim, the hospice chaplain, rushed in. In a hurry, as usual, she still managed to look very elegant. Jill thought it was the carefully ironed silk or linen clothes she always wore.

Michal Poe

"Hi, Jill," she greeted. "I'm here to pick up my protestant type vestments. Hope I haven't misplaced them again."

Jill took Kim aside and explained the volunteer showdown thing so that Kim wouldn't interrupt Dean's experiment.

"Why didn't he do that in his office?" Kim asked.

Dean heard that and wrote on a notepad, then handed it to Donna, who was nearby. She looked up from her billing work long enough to hand it to Jill, who handed it to Kim. He'd written, "Part of experiment is that it's public!" Jill shrugged and Kim shook her head.

Kim went to the supply closet and found the shawl collar she needed. Kim kept various accouterments for her ministrations and funerals. As a nondenominational hospice chaplain, she needed quite a variety of articles.

Within that small space were the implements Kim insisted were necessary for her protean assignments. Organized—or crammed, some might say—were: bells, gongs, brass bowls, empty vases and urns, chant books, prayer flags and papers, candles, Korans, Torah readings, Bibles, crosses, and pentacles, as well as vials of incense, honey, raw sugar, and mineral salts. Another shelf contained headscarves, yarmulkes, robes, prayer shawls, and other vestments. In various boxes were several hats, including a top hat. Another shelf contained picture frames, guest books, feathers, recorders, an Indian flute, two autoharps, and several CDs. Also, there was an old but very workable boom box, a megaphone, and sheet music. In the corner, there stood a few walking sticks. Next there were boxes and boxes of FUNERAL labels. Kim passed these out to funeral attendees for the procession to the graveyards. Behind those was a wooden container labeled Blanks, which were used for military gun salutes. Several small American flags were kept in that box too. On the very top shelf, an empty animal cage was wedged in sideways.

Kim once said she thought of taking the time to write Funerals for Dummies to keep in the supply closet, but she figured that'd probably already been done. Everyone had laughed as they imagined the car crash dummy in a coffin on the book's cover picture.

Kim used the small step stool, seemingly found what else she needed, and stopped by in front of Jill's work area, catching Jill as she was about to leave.

"Jill, I wanted to tell you that I just came back from Rita Stark's home. She and Davis need you out there. He wants reassurance that he's doing the right thing. He was in tears when I left. It's a toss-up whether you or Michelle would be best, but since it was mostly nursing questions, I picked you."

"I'll see if I can rearrange my schedule." Jill always paid attention to Kim's requests because they were spot on. Some of the volunteers or other worker's evaluations would be way off the mark. Jill would rush out only to find everything was "super duper and gosh, we really wanted to take a nap but had to wait up for you." That type of comment was always disappointing, especially after all of Jill's effort.

"Also," Kim asked, "is there any way you can get to the Bense funeral? It's at three. I don't know a thing about them and there's no one else to conduct the service. You must know something."

"Mr. Bense? That man was only in the program for two days, Kim. I only saw him once."

"Well, you could fake it and add something personal to the service about him, couldn't you?"

That was the second time she'd heard "fake it" this morning, but she answered, "I'll try to make it. I'll try to think of something."

"I'll leave the directions on your machine. Thanks." Kim spoke over her shoulder on the way out.

Jill had called her scheduled early afternoon visit, the one that needed the O2 meter. It was easily put off until tomorrow, since there was no urgent need. She took the meter anyway so she could use it for Rita Stark.

***

Whereas Jill's own mom had good physical health, but her mind was gone, Rita's mind stayed as sharp as ever, but her body was gone. She was in her early fifties. However, she was in the last stages of ALS, Lou Gehrig's disease. The newest and youngest nurse, Lane March, had begged Jill to take this patient when the name and diagnosis had come up several months ago. Jill had agreed. Sandy had told Jill later that was a mistake. "Your halo is getting tighter and tighter, cutting off the blood to your brain," she'd said. But as she told Sandy, she didn't do it for Lane's sake, because Lane needed to extend her expertise and not discriminate against those who were dying "harshly," as the young nurse had so succinctly expressed it. Jill did it for Rita's sake.

It was a very tough assignment to most eyes, but an inspiration to Jill in many ways. Jill felt lucky to get to know Rita. The first time Jill visited, Rita had been able to speak in short, quiet sentences. Even when she could only whisper, Rita loved to converse, and she always tried to keep Jill there as long as she could. Rita had become more and more isolated, which was a shame because she was a very interesting person.

Rita had run marathons for over thirty years. She was able to offer Jill some incentive when Jill became serious about trying to resume running for exercise. Jill had always been very active and had recently added a few lavender fields to her farm She wanted to capture the younger demographic. She kept busy, but she was not in good aerobic health. She honestly had never been able to fit in gym time because of her home responsibilities. So running seemed like the perfect thing. There were plenty of small hills around Jill's area. Jill hadn't wanted to run over the hills, thinking she needed to start on flatlands. That would entail driving somewhere, and that didn't work out at all. So her running program never got off the ground—until Rita. She'd let Jill know that the hilly type of terrain was ideal. She gave Jill practical tips: how to avoid injuries, good dietary ideas, and how to stay motivated until the running became the prime motivation for running. Jill was grateful.

After Rita had been on the program for a month or so, Jill alerted Donna, who supervised the volunteers, and Donna was able to get someone to come out to Rita's home. That volunteer, Anne, was sent mainly for socialization. After getting to know Rita, Anne helped write down Rita's running experiences. Then Anne edited the essay to the point where they felt they could send the unsolicited article to a running magazine, and the article was published. This did so much in boosting Rita's spirits.

Rita's husband, Davis, was very proud of her. He, too, had become a runner. He'd told Jill it probably saved his life, because he hadn't realized that heart disease ran in his family. In the past five years, he'd seen two of his brothers die at an early age from coronary thromboses.

Now, inside Rita's house, Jill could see she wasn't doing well. It was getting to the point where she didn't have the strength in her lungs to breathe properly. When Jill checked Rita, she found that even with her new oxygen mask on, rather than the previous cannula, the meter showed the O2 level was too low. Soon Rita would not have the strength to breathe. Jill took Davis aside after making sure that Rita was as comfortable as humanly possible.

"Davis," she said, "you know the time is close."

"I know," he said, as he began to tear up. "Is there anything else I can do for her?"

Jill knew that giving him a small task would help him feel he was helping Rita more. Davis was very much on board with the hospice philosophy. He didn't want to hasten her death, but he didn't want to prolong her suffering either. Jill normalized Rita's end time signs and symptoms and then gave Davis an assignment.

"Davis, see this package of disposable sponges here that the bath aide left? I want you to add a little non-alcoholic mouthwash to some water and put a teeny bit of the solution on the sponge. Now you can run the sponge around the inside of her mouth and over her teeth."

Davis got the mouthwash and made up a cup of solution. He watched as Jill temporarily removed Rita's oxygen mask and demonstrated the procedure once. Then he tried it, and he was able to get Rita's mouth fresh. Jill could tell it was the right thing to do, because he settled down and looked pleased. Jill continued to explain what was going on with his wife's symptoms and the procedure to follow at the time of death. This comforted him.

Then Jill spoke to Rita as if she were fully capable and aware. Jill chose her words with care. "Rita, hospice will follow up on your family and look out for Davis. You'll never know how much knowing you has helped me. Thank you for that. You're so…encouraging. All the hospice nurses who have seen you tell me what a special place you have in their heart. Goodbye, brave traveler, good journey to you, Rita."

Rita was too weak to answer, but when Jill leaned down and gave her a kiss on the forehead and an ever so gentle hug, Jill sensed Rita knew that the time was close. As hard as it was to let this lovely woman go, somehow Jill felt at peace and perceived the warmth of light surrounding Rita.

Jill paused at the doorway on her way out. There she let Davis know the death might possibly happen today. She had to hold Davis for some time. It was just a long hug, and though it was something simple, Jill knew it was meaningful.

***

After her visit, and before she could get to the funeral, she listened to her many phone messages, with her speaker on. Nine messages in one hour. Only three were important. The first savable one was from Bill Dobson's son, or son-in-law, Jill couldn't tell. Dobson was a new patient, and Jill didn't know where that case was going. There were many family members involved, but mostly in only a superficial way. The patient, though a nice man, was usually "upset" as he called it. He would probably need a lot of attention, at least initially. Jill put him on her Tuesday schedule. She wrote down the directions to the Bense funeral that Kim had just left her. Then she received a call from Fern, Stina's caregiver at the day care home.

She flipped off her speakerphone. It wasn't often that Fern called her at work.

"Nothing urgent," Fern said. "I just need to talk to you. Could you, rather than Jason, pick up Stina this evening?"

Hmm, Jill thought, that didn't sound good, on more than one level.

"Okay, Fern I'll pick Mom up, but I'll have to get there a little late tonight."

"Great," Fern answered. "Bye."

Jill always noticed Fern was so cheerful, so Jill added, "Have a nice day." She honestly didn't know where that phrase, have a nice day, came from. It sounded hackneyed. But it was too late to add anything further anyway, as Fern had already hung up.

Jill also had received a message from her fellow nurse, Lane March. It was a plea for Jill to bring the oxygen meter back to the office. "Please, Jill, I have an open to do, and the doctor said it was essential to get a reading for this man. I need it as soon as possible!"

***

Once more, Jill made a trip back to the office. It was only a little past one, but the day already seemed endless. Richard, Stuart, and Dean were still there in the workroom. They were all in the same little chairs. But now, Stuart was grimacing and sitting crooked. Richard, on the other hand, was still stiff and straight, with his poor attempt at an open posture. He also had a very determined look on his face. They'd been there for over two hours, and Jill's back hurt just looking at them. She got a small wave from Dean as he looked at his watch and made a quick observation note on his writing pad.

Donna eagerly took the O2 meter from Jill, saying, "I'll clean it for you, Jill, and make sure Lane gets it. Sorry you had to come all the way back. Don't worry about the guys… I'm about ready to give them bathroom breaks."

"I'm not just worried about the volunteers."

"I know, but Dean said it invigorates him, knowing he may be adding something to the scientific community."

"That's true of him," Jill said. "He's so careful. I bet he'll find something good to write about."

"The nice thing about a theory, if you test it correctly, is this: even if it turns out wrong, you still get a paper out of it. I did a good one in my undergraduate days. It turned out that none of my hypothesis held up. The professor quoted Winston Churchill a lot to motivate us. The one I remember goes something like, 'Success is meeting failure with enthusiasm.'"

"There's a fine line between that and denial," Jill commented. She looked up from arranging her nursing bag. "What was it on?"

"What?"

"Your paper. What was it on?"

"I wish I remembered. It was something that was cutting edge at the time. I do recall that the title was enigmatic: 'Id repression and its effect on the ego.' I may have the words reversed though," Donna chuckled. "I'll have to dig it out sometime. I was so full of myself then, even wanted to go into politics."

"You'd be great in politics." Jill stood up to leave. "But I'm glad you ended up here."

Michal Poe

"I hope it's not the end," Donna said, with all sincerity, and a smile too so Jill would know that she wasn't offended. "By the way is Goulden on service?"

"Yes. Apparently it was his Dad that stole his medical card. The son had found his father twenty years ago, through a private detective. His father, with the same name was homeless, yet in good health and a perfectly self-satisfied man who wanted nothing to do with his son."

"Those stories do turn out like that, sometimes."

"I guess through the years Goulden had anonymously sent his father large money orders to help him through life, even though his dad had tried to clean out his bank accounts, and used his name to get fancy hotels in various cities."

"Our patient had the money to do all that?"

"Oh yeah. He'd never pressed charges. He simply paid off what was due."

"Usually it's the younger taking advantage of the older. We always get new twists."

"We do."

Jill had wanted to be on time but saw, during her drive, that she might be a tad late to the Bense funeral. She was still having second thoughts about her attendance. Part of it was the embarrassment of not remembering one of her patients. That didn't seem right. She also wondered if she was neglecting any of her regular patients by using the time for the funeral. Perhaps one of them could use an extra visit. But Kim had pleaded and really wanted her there. So she was off to see if her presence would be helpful at the funeral of someone she couldn't even recall.

Those who signed up and died quickly were hard for Jill to keep straight. The average time in hospice care was usually only a month or so. Many patients and their families, thought signing up for that kind of care meant giving up. So they only signed on when death was very near and comfort was paramount. Or sometimes the family was tired of the hospitalization and they knew that the patient wanted a quiet death in the home. From the day the patient was signed into hospice, a nurse could come to the home after the death and take care of the paperwork. This step was useful for the families and saved a lot of grief too, because in most cases and communities, it meant bypassing the coroner coming out to the home. It also stopped the need for autopsies and all the rest of the red tape that might come from home deaths that weren't officially expected.

If the illness progressed to the point where doctors said the patient's time was limited, why not get good health care and comfort? That was Jill's bottom line.

Though hospice care was helpful for the families, it was hard for everyone to wrap their mind around the actual impending death. Jill saw what a struggle it was. Taking another staff member along on the first visit took some of the burden off the nurse. It provided another voice to help explain hospice. Sometimes, their doctor hadn't properly prepared the patient or family. More often they'd been informed and agreed, yet the idea of impending death didn't fully register.

Checking her watch, Jill found she would be ten or fifteen minutes late to the chapel. As she neared, she realized this was the same place she'd been to a few weeks ago, when Kim officiated at Jim's funeral.

Occasionally the hospice program had to kick a few patients out because they got better. The term used was *graduating the patient.* Jill had graduated a few patients, and it didn't always go smoothly. Some were upset because they felt they had good care in hospice and wanted that to continue even if the doctor said they were no longer considered terminal. Jim had been incorrectly diagnosed and was happy to sign off the program after finding his kidney disease had reversed itself. He'd put all his affairs in order and then felt he'd been given a reprieve. He was a different man, in a totally different place, when he re-signed onto hospice five years later. This time it was a true prognosis. Jill really liked that man. She'd liked his funeral too.

***

When she arrived at the chapel, she tried to slip in without being seen since the funeral was in progress. Jill sensed by the mood emanating from the sparsely attended affair that it might be headed toward disaster. Most everyone was sitting in the back rows, but even there, there was still plenty of room. Jill always tried to sit way back. It was helpful if you had to leave early. Placed at the end of each bench were new boxes of tissue. Jill noticed that not one person was dabbing at their eyes.

Up on the podium, Kim was leaving long pauses between words. When she spied Jill, she brightened perceptibly, and immediately exclaimed, "There's Dr. Bense's hospice nurse. I'm sure you'd like to hear her give a short talk."

Jill smiled outwardly but inwardly thought, *All right, Kim, now you really owe me*. The open casket was sitting in the aisle. Jill had never seen a coffin positioned in the aisle. It was almost as if the casket was too heavy and the deceased was just plunked there. Or maybe it was some kind of religious thing that Jill had never experienced.

On the way up to the podium, she found that when she neared the casket, she had to actually turn sideways to squeeze by. She remembered that the deceased was indeed a heavyset man. The casket was oversize, but most were these days. The manufacturers of caskets claimed the prices were going up because the population was getting bigger and heavier. Yet seeing someone so large was different for Jill, because most hospice patients eventually lost a lot of weight before they died.

Jill figured she could give a very short talk. A night nurse had pronounced Bense's death. Jill could remember patients better if she was the one who came to the home after the patient died. She was always very observant then, and writing up the final paperwork a second time brought it home and solidified the person in her mind.

After a slow walk to the podium, Jill had to say something.

She settled on, "I'd like you to know how pleased I was to serve Dr. Bense." She hadn't even known he was a doctor. Maybe a Ph.D., she decided.

Now she recalled he had a lot of books in his home. She continued, "How I enjoyed seeing all the books in his home. I would like to give condolences to the family whom Dr. Bense loved." She ended by saying, "Most people die the way they live. I so enjoyed having him as a patient."

She realized she'd already said the last line in the beginning. It hadn't made any difference because no one was listening anyway. She could look down from the podium and see that some were text messaging, some were writing checks, and some were apparently making to do or grocery lists. Kim looked pleased; she had extended the short service a little while, and she could use Jill's little talk to begin the wrap up.

Michal Poe

"Thank you. Jill Wheaten was the nurse who so enjoyed serving this family…and was impressed by his many shelves of books. This concludes the formal part of the service."

Some people thought the funeral was over and were getting up to leave. Kim quickly added, "I know so many people have been affected by Dr. Bense's life. I would like to ask anyone who wishes to speak to come up and tell us a little story about your relationship with Dr. Bense." The couple about to leave promptly sat down.

Kim waited expectantly. There were no takers. She added, with enthusiasm, "Just a short little story, since so many of you seem so touched." That was followed by an equally embarrassing silence.

In desperation Kim looked at the widow, "Mrs. Bense?" Mrs. Bense shook her head no, in a very firm manner.

Fortunately, Kim knew how to cover. "Well, people seem to be shy, but I know you have many good memories to hold in your heart. Let's now sing the closing hymn, number 268, which is also printed on the notices given as you arrived." She said this with a big smile and nod toward the Bense coffin. She lifted her hands as those assembled reluctantly rummaged around to find the handout before they stood up.

They began to sing a dirge-like tune, with no musical accompaniment. The words to the song may have seemed appropriate earlier, but they now sounded hollow. Kim did have a lovely voice though. The only words Jill paid attention to (and only because it was so ironic) were, "We will know them by their deeds, and tell of wondrous things."

Some funeral homes used the time during the last hymn to close the casket. Two men in black suits came forward to accomplish this task. They had a certain formal way of doing this, but they were hampered by the tight fit between the pews. As they were struggling with the closing, Mrs. Bense, hymnal in hand, walked over and pulled down the wooden staffs holding the coffin open, and the lid slammed down by itself.

Jill winced. She was worried about Dr. Bense's fingers being caught in the latch or something. Plus, even with the singing it made a very loud sound.

Unfazed, Mrs. Bense went back to her bench and finished up the song.

The whole scene made Jill sad. She knew nothing about Dr. Bense's private life. But didn't anyone deserve better than this? This funeral was a good example of why not to have a funeral. Then again, for Jill, it had been a sad day anyway. She had to give Kim a stern look, as she could tell that Kim, at first amazed at what had just happened, was now trying to suppress a laugh.

Jill didn't have time to reconnoiter with Kim after the funeral. She saw Kim rubbing her head again and thought, *I'll bet it's those headaches*. Nevertheless, Kim had certainly been in top form during the funeral, even as disastrous as it seemed. Anyway, who wouldn't get headaches with the job Kim had? But because of Kim's normal, easygoing personality, Jill saw that Kim never saw how work wore on her. She knew Kim had been undergoing extensive medical testing lately. Jill hoped whatever they found was fixable.

Kim always said how much she loved her job and wouldn't consider anything different. The nurses, all very adept themselves, were in awe of Kim's multitasking abilities. Jill once told Kim she had excellent emotional peripheral vision. Kim had loved that compliment. But it was the truth. Kim always handled her patients and families so beautifully, even, as it seemed during this funeral, under the most potentially embarrassing situations.

Jill thought Kim had an envious home life. She'd been married to the same man, her first marriage, for ten years. Her husband, Brent, was an architect, now with his own business. He was a very meticulous man who loved his family. Kim went home to order and love and fun. Brent had told Jill that Kim was the center of his world. That was easy to see. Kim was a wonderful stepparent for Brent's teens—a usually thankless but, this time, well-appreciated role.

After her little past talks with Jill about getting worn out, Kim began to meet with Dean to talk about her stress in a semi-official therapy. Jill knew he was such a good listener and that must have helped. Dean and Kim had to have a close working relationship. The two of them worked together with the families after the death of a patient, so it was important they stay abreast of each other's interventions. The hospice families were followed officially for a full year. The nurse, except in a small way at times, stepped out of the picture after the death. But for those two, the staff knew it was harder to establish an end date.

Leaving the funeral, Jill received a silent beep with the office number displayed with an exclamation point after it. She called the office immediately. Dean answered the phone, so apparently the volunteer standoff had reached some kind of conclusion. She received the urgent news from Dean that Rita had just died and Davis had asked if Jill could go and be there.

Jill took a moment to collect her thoughts, and then she put her Jeep in gear and drove back to Rita's home to do the death pronouncement.

Jill - Hospice Nurse, Book Two: Last Exit

***

Davis was very ebullient. His first words were, "She went home. She's whole again."

That relief at first was very normal. Jill knew that even the next few days, although emotional, would be caught up in planning details, calls, and family interaction. Then there would be the difficult weeks, months, and even years. That was going to be the hard part—getting used to living without a person physically being there. Grief was individual, dependent upon many things. Some bereaved would tell Jill, "I want him/her back, I don't care how sick he/she was, this is too difficult." But for now, yes, Rita was free of her broken body, and Jill was as much pleased about that as Davis was.

After Jill made all the necessary calls, she set about destroying the medicine. She mixed it in her small, cat-litter-filled bags to avoid flushing it down into the water system. She put that bag inside another and threw it in the trash. Then Jill sat down at the dining room table to do her paperwork. She knew this would take a while, as she sensed Davis needed to talk. Jill would have to let Donna know that she could fax the final paperwork and give her schedule for tomorrow from home in about an hour or so. That wasn't really the normal procedure. Management liked the staff to begin and end their day in the office. But this move would save overtime. Jill knew that since the budget was very lean this time of year, management would allow this deviation.

"Jill," Davis said, after sitting in the chair across the table from her, "I have to tell you what happened right after you left. I came back into the room, and after a little while, Rita's eyes fluttered and she sighed, and it looked like she was trying to talk. So I took off her mask for a minute and I leaned down right to her. It was amazing. She could just barely whisper, and it took her a while, but do you know what she said?"

"No," Jill answered. "Please tell me."

Davis spoke, slowly just as Rita would have, "She said, 'Honey.' You know her voice was hoarse, but she said, 'I was running. In my dream…running.' Then, Jill," Davis continued, sounding as if he was still in awe over what had happened, "She smiled. Jill, that was the first time I saw her smile in a month. I was crying. A tear ran down her face too. I kissed her and held her and soon after that she stopped breathing. Right there in my arms, the way it had to be."

"Davis." Jill said.

"Right in my arms, and she's running now, I know it…" Davis began to cry.

Jill stayed in her chair and didn't offer him a tissue or come and hug him to interrupt his emotions. He needed to savor this time, and so did Jill.

While they waited for the mortuary, Jill suggested that it would be good to have someone come there to sit with him. He'd called a friend to come and stay the night. This made Jill feel better.

As was sometimes the case, when there were such heartfelt emotions, it was hard for her to go. But when the mortuary people arrived, she left.

Back in her vehicle, she took the cellophane off her new journal and made her first entry:

Rita. Running Free
Goodbye earth.
A peaceful life of a million steps.
Remembered well, by those she left.

***

Jill - Hospice Nurse, Book Two: Last Exit

Before Jill went to pick up her mother, she made a quick stop for a few groceries. She tried to keep the shopping up so she could have more free time on the weekends for her new side business, Garden Enterprises. The trend around the bigger cities was reverting back to small organic truck farming or other land use. In the area where Jill now lived, these sorts of enterprises were thriving. One of her neighbors had a Christmas tree farm, and Jill's own new lavender fields were beginning to do well. She was serious about her avocation, wanting it to be a cushion for retirement in her later years. It also gave her time outside. She was a farm girl at heart.

Six years ago, when her current property had come up for sale, Jill had finally gotten far enough up her career ladder, making good pay, so she was able to buy the land. It had always been a dream of hers. Perhaps she romanticized her mother's childhood on a real working farm. She loved the stories her mother told about her childhood. Mixed farming, it was called then, before agribusiness had taken over in the Midwest. When Jill and her brother, C.J., were children, Stina had a small truck garden. She didn't make much profit, but it was enough to supplement the government check she received because her husband had been killed in combat, and she'd never remarried.

Jill had learned a lot about farming from her mom during the first few years her mother lived with her. But, Jill now realized, even then, five or six years ago, Stina was becoming slightly confused at times. But no one paid attention to the signs then. They were easy to gloss over. They'd both had fun while she and Stina laid out the ideas for the use of the land and drew up the plans. The first thing they did was tilled the ground and planted their own garden. All that first fall, every day was an adventure as Stina found and invented different recipes using their own produce. The past three years Jill had had a medicinal herb garden right outside her kitchen. Her mother had begun a book for the uses of the plants. She hadn't finished it, but Jill knew there was enough information to write up a little blurb to go with each packet of herbs she planned on selling. That task was on Jill's things to be done list.

Walking around the grocery store, she picked up the few items she needed. This was the store where she usually shopped. She knew the aisles by heart and didn't have to think. Jill was feeling very nostalgic. Some of her best times from her childhood were with her mother while they were grocery shopping. Their budget was always tight, but her mother could really stretch a dollar and produce wonderful means from scratch. The chopping, the boiling of bones for stock, the endless array of spices covering every counter, the prep work, and the thought that her mother put into meals, was an art Jill couldn't duplicate.

After Stina had moved in with Jill, she began to do the cooking again, and the meals had been marvelous. Stina had looked in Jill's freezer after her first shopping expedition and she was aghast. The freezer kind of looked like that again, now that her mom couldn't cook or even understand what she was eating.

Okay, Jill could admit she didn't like to cook, but she still felt a little guilty as she picked up the canned refried beans and the frozen enchiladas and placed them in her basket. Her Mom had always been very careful about what she put in her own body too. When she'd turned forty, Jill began to think it might be good to take better care of her own health, even though she did like frozen dinners. The new eating habits were a big change, and a good one, but she had to admit she was making a slow start. She headed toward the produce section, motivating herself by thinking Jason might pick up some good habits for his future. She bought ingredients for stir-fry.

Jill stuck the groceries on the floor of the backseat. She couldn't put things in the hatch, as they would get mixed up with her nursing supplies. The next stop was the day care home. Jill grabbed her large-toothed comb out of the glove box and took a few swipes at her hair. She smiled into the rearview mirror, then caught herself because she realized she was nervous about this meeting.

Fern met her at the door. "Jill," she said, "Thanks for coming."

"Yes," Jill replied, while being ushered into the front parlor.

"Now don't be upset, Jill, but your mother has had a big change today."

"Huh?" Jill asked. "What?"

"We've had to diaper her. Her accidents are increasing, and the cleanup is confusing and hard on her. We decided, if it's okay with you, of course, to keep her diapered at all times. I have the pull-up type on her, and she doesn't even know the difference."

"Ahh," Jill said, feeling very much relieved. "Thank you, Fern. I'm sure you're right. She's been having more accidents at home too. I've been putting a lot of pads on her bed. But this is the best solution."

"You knew it was coming, right, Jill?" Fern asked in a very compassionate way.

"Yes, but every change is wrenching."

"That's why I wanted to tell you first—more of a woman's thing. At seventeen, Jason's a little young for this."

"He's doing fine on dropping her off and picking her up, though?"

"Oh, yes, he does very well. He's always a gentleman and right on time. Stina brightens up when she sees him. She always says, 'Where have you been? I've been waiting for you.' Sometimes she shines through."

As if on cue, Stina appeared, leaning on her walker in the doorway, and said to Jill, "Where have you been? I've been waiting for you."

Jill accepted a few nights' supply of diapers, noting she'd have to pick some more up in the morning. She securely buckled her mom into the passenger side seatbelt.

***

She arrived home as Jason pulled up. He still had the big old Chevy Caprice convertible that had been left to Jill after her divorce. She had passed it down to her son. He was emotionally outgrowing it and no longer wanted to spend any money to make it fun. He was upset about all the money spent on gas for it too. He was looking into a part-time job in order to get a fast, hot car. He and Jill had gone round and round about him working. Jill didn't want him to get a job. He was bright, made excellent grades, and was into sports. And frankly, sometimes Jill needed him home. It was still an issue.

"Mom! Grandma!" he enthused and ran over to give each one a big hug. That boy was so charming, Jill thought, just like his father. Fortunately, he also had a very serious side, similar to her own. He was lucky, she mused, to have gotten the best from both parents. Anyway, she was ever so proud of him, and he knew it.

Jill made the stir-fry and had to admit it was a good dinner. Afterward, Jason washed up the dishes while she led her mother out to the small, partially enclosed front porch. She ensconced her mom in the rocking chair. It was the one constant piece of furniture Stina, and then Jill, had been able to continue taking from place to place. It was a big arts and crafts type rocker, with wide armrests and a leather seat that had been recovered numerous times. Her Mom had been given that rocker years ago by a neighbor who was moving. This was right after Jill's older brother, C.J., was born and before Stina's husband decided to join the military. Her Mom had told Jill that she'd been surprised her husband had done that, because she knew he was a conscientious objector. But Stina relayed he was also worried about getting drafted, as it'd happened to a few of his friends; this was the Vietnam era. Clifford knew that by voluntarily joining the service he could get good training. "He was such a kind man," her mom said—always describing him that way.

The sun was setting. Jill and Stina were quiet. Jill sat on the step and drank her hot tea. The porch looked out over the lavender plantings. The property was triangular shaped. Jill's little home was on one corner; the fields took up much of the rest of the property. Her vegetable garden was on the opposite corner was where the main road passed. It received a lot of traffic. That's where Jill planned on building a slant-roofed, shed enclosure to sell her products.

Her mom began to rock in her chair. The rhythm and the slight noise of the rockers against the wooden porch were comforting. Jill had a theory about rocking chairs.

Michal Poe

She thought a one-size-fits-all type of therapy would be to build a big rocking chair and then have her clients climb into her lap. Without a word beyond shush and a few pats, she would rock a person's psychological concerns back into their proper place. She'd have to find a clinical-sounding name for it, but she knew it'd work.

Tonight Jill thought the saddest thing she'd have to rock away was the fact that Stina had forgotten her husband Clifford. He'd been the love of Stina's life. He'd died very late in the Vietnam War, so many years ago.

It always seemed the saddest thing.

She went to the side of her mom's chair, sat on the wide armrest, and put her arm around her mother's shoulders. She patted her a few times. Stina didn't acknowledge her presence. She was in her own world as usual. Jill was somewhere else as well.

After putting Stina to bed, Jill got busy again. She faxed the paperwork to Donna's number at the office, straightened the house a bit, and then did a quick pass through her car, removing all the papers and trash accumulated during the day. If she didn't clean it out often, it soon looked lived in.

She gave a knock on Jason's door. When she entered, she knew better than to say anything about the hurricane condition of his room. That wasn't one of the battles in which she chose to engage. The hard part was allowing him to suffer the consequences of, say, not being able to find a clean shirt because the clean and dirty laundry was all in a pile in a corner. He thrived, so things were adequate to his own needs. Jason was reading while sitting on the floor with his back against his bed.

Jill carefully used her foot to push aside a pile of papers and sat on the floor with another cup of tea and explained to Jason about the diapers.

"Mom," he said, "I love Grandma and would do anything for her, but I don't think I could do that."

"I know, son," Jill said as she reached over and squeezed his hand. "I'll take care of that. Also I've begun to think we could use a little more help around the house, you know, maybe on the weekends."

"Whatever you think, Mom, as long as they stay out of my room."

Jill smiled at his comment.

Jason jumped up as if he he'd suddenly remembered something. He pulled out several brochures from his backpack. Jill thought it might be more dementia information, but it was college applications. He excitedly showed the schools he and his counselor thought he'd not only be able to get into but also get partial scholarships. Jill was pleased until she saw that all the brochures were for universities on the East Coast. Thousands of miles away.

"But Jason," she said, trying to keep her voice level, "I thought maybe you'd find a nice school around here, or at least one that was no more than a day's drive."

"Heck no, Mom," Jason answered. "I'm going to the best school we can afford. They're all in New York and New Jersey. Oh, and there's a good one in Massachusetts."

Until this very moment, Jill had never thought about empty nest syndrome. In fact, she didn't even believe in such a thing. But was this slight wrenching of her gut the beginnings of separation from her son? Come to think of it, she'd been having this strange dream lately. In it, she was a rutabaga plant and someone was trying to prune her by cutting off her roots. A sharp shovel was plunged into the earth, hit and miss. This hadn't worked—it only made the plant real easy to rip out of the ground. She'd woken up very disturbed after that dream, having no idea what it was about. That is, until now.

    She forced a smile. "Well, you really are thinking ahead. Since it's a ways away, we have time to think about it. Good for you."

    "Less than a year. The counselor told me the due date for the applications comes up soon. The better schools have a big a screening process. Sherrice's dad, Rob, knows about this too. He went to MIT or Princeton or…I forget. But he says those Ivy League schools are the best the place to go."

    Sherrice was Jason's girlfriend. She was his first serious girlfriend, and Jill really liked her. She was quiet and sensible. She and Jason made a cute couple. Jill didn't know if it would last. She wasn't jealous. She didn't think no one was good enough for her son. She prided herself on that. But the thing that riled her now was Sherrice's dad. He almost seemed to be stepping into a father's role. Jason, of course, hardly ever saw Chris, his own father. Jill's only sibling, her brother, C.J., lived out of state. Although he tried to keep up with Jason's life, he had a family of his own. Jill had been father and mother to Jason. Jill had heard Rob's name too often lately. And this redistribution of alliance toward Sherrice's father really bothered her. So far she'd kept those thoughts to herself.

    "We still have some time, Jason. We'll talk a lot more this weekend about these things, okay?"

"Right, Mom," Jason said, fortunately not sensing her mood this time. "Need anything else before I finish my homework?"

"No. Thanks, son," Jill answered. "I'm going to go for a long run though. See you later."

Jill changed into her running clothes. She hadn't had time to get her home messages, so while she changed she listened to her answering machine. There was nothing important, except the last one from her boyfriend. "Hi, Jill. Bennett here. Listen, I know we had a thing for this weekend, but I'm going to be going out of town, so call me and we'll talk. Bye."

That didn't sound good. Since her divorce over ten years ago, Bennett was her first real boyfriend, or male companion, or slightly significant other. Or whatever it was called these days. True, he admitted he'd been bisexual at one phase of his life, and he and Jill sometimes laughed about how friends had set them up on a blind date in order to scare him straight. He was a little older and on the quiet side, had really good manners, and was wealthy besides. He was good with her and Jason, and with Stina too. He had a busy life, with his dental specialty entailing lots of emergency root canals and such. He lived a ways away, and that made their time together a little scarce. Jill had liked that part of it. She was new at allowing others into her life, and she thought it worked out well for both of them. But lately, she'd noticed it seemed as if he was pulling away a bit. He'd even politely criticized her for her lack of passion. That hurt, but she would never pretend to be something she wasn't. Not anymore, she'd decided. Early on in their relationship, she found herself tending to go back to her old habits of trying to fit herself into the other's agenda. So this honesty, this self-assurance, included her never professing to being in love until she was sure. She'd made that mistake more than once in the past and perhaps was being a little over-cautious. But if the feelings were not there, she wouldn't force it. As she'd pointed out to Bennett, it had been almost ten years since she'd had any kind of relationship.

She couldn't face the implications of that phone message now. She headed into the clear, darkening, inviting outdoors and began to run.

Run she did. Up and down the hills just as Rita had recommended. Faster and faster and farther and farther, with tears streaming down and flying off her face she ran. She ran to process her losses. She ran to find her breath. She ran to assuage her sadness. She ran and cried until she realized it was the longest run in quite a while and she felt freer. "Thank you, Rita," she exclaimed out loud, still crying as she looked up at the new evening's stars, "Thank you."

TUESDAY

The next morning Jill called Bennett.

"Jill, dear," he said. "I know you'll be disappointed about the change of plans."

"Well," Jill asked, "Bennett, are you doing okay?"

"Tell you what, I'll come by Tuesday night and we'll talk."

"That's tonight."

"Tonight around seven then? Okay, see you then."

Jill had to settle for that. She was right to have noticed the strain in their relationship over the past few weeks. They'd both let things drift. She hung up feeling lonely already.

Shoving thoughts of Bennett aside, Jill sighed and tapped on her mother's door, waiting a few seconds before opening it.

"Mom? Time to get ready."

Jill was easily able to change and diaper her mom. It was almost effortless, certainly far less trouble than cleaning up accidents. The pull-ups were clever. Stina really didn't note any difference between them and her usual underwear. Jill was so thankful for Fern's care and knowledge. She was learning a lot from her about how to manage her mom and still keep Stina's dignity intact.

Jill smiled as Jason loaded up his car and pretended to be a limousine operator. Jason kept a light attitude with his grandma and made a game out any situation. It always worked well. Stina called Jason by his name sometimes, and other times she called him her driver. Jason bowed and positioned her in the back seat. That's where Stina had to ride now, in his car. It was safest with her back there, because Jason had taken the inside handles off the doors. She had less to fiddle with and couldn't get in as much trouble. They'd had to take this precaution after the last time she'd sat in the front seat. Stina had opened the door on the freeway and tried to get out of her seatbelt.

There comes a point where you just aren't comfortable in denial. In fact, it may be dangerous to stay in that state. That was the defining moment for Jill. She and Jason started attending the dementia support group religiously. Jill had learned that it was helpful for Stina to have something to hold in her hands most of the time. That way she would be fiddling with the object she was holding, rather then other things in her environment. This morning Stina was holding her hat, since Jill noted it was a little nippy outside.

As he was settling Stina in, Jason asked Jill, "Mom, is it alright if Sherrice comes over for dinner tonight?"

"Absolutely fine," she answered, pleased that he'd asked.

Even though Stina's behavior was getting worse, her care, thanks to Fern's clues and Stina's lessened physical strength, was more manageable these days. Jill knew this was the time when Stina was turning inward, just as the literature said. She no longer had the wherewithal to interact appropriately with her surroundings.

Jill was pleased her mother still found some things that appeared to make her happy. She was always able to recognize Jill and usually recognized Jason. True, Stina didn't recognize any others, and even when she was shown pictures of Clifford her expression was blank. Jill was a teenager before she heard the full story of her dad's death. She'd only known that he'd joined the navy, trained as a corpsman, and was placed as a medic with the marines. So he was always in the thick of battle.

When Jill's brother, C.J., had turned eighteen, he'd looked up and found some of their dad's old buddies. Yes, he found that Clifford had died with valor and was a hero. But these men, these former brothers in arms, also told another story. While on a night watch, Clifford and another man were on the periphery of the hamlet they were protecting, and they wandered a bit too far. Suddenly, in silence, they were attacked. They were so close, the vegetation was so thick, and the night so dark, that no one could draw a weapon. They used hand-to-hand combat. Clifford and his buddy survived. They went back to camp, told their senior officer what had happened, and, because they didn't want to draw more enemy to the area, the officer waited till morning to go to the scene to see if the bodies were still there. There they found two dead enemy combatants. Their necks were broken, their knives were still in their sheaths, and a few undischarged hand grenades were on the ground near them. The dead looked to be about thirteen or fourteen years old. One of Clifford's buddies said Clifford was never the same again. He said Clifford had always been fearless, but now he was reckless. He repeatedly faced enemy fire to rescue wounded combatants in his unit. The last time, right before the war was over, he'd pulled four wounded marines out of the line of fire, getting them to safety in a helicopter before he was shot down. He was twenty-three years old.

Michal Poe

C.J. was two and Stina was pregnant with Jill at the time. C.J. kept his dad's posthumous Navy Cross for valor pinned in a velvet shadow box. It was prominently displayed in the entryway of his home.

Jill recognized that she and her brother had really lost both their parents now. The final blow for Jill was when Stina couldn't garden anymore. All that she had taught Jill was gone from her mind. Fern told Jill that Stina would sit for hours next to the raised beds they had in the back yard and run her hands through the warm dirt, smiling all the while.

She wanted Jason to feel comfortable about having people back in the home. She and Jason had become a little isolated the past few years. So she shook off her thoughts and added, for Jason's sake, before he left the driveway, "Any ideas about what we'll make to eat tonight?"

"You could get a pizza at that new place since you're picking up Grandma."

"Great. I'll order a few salads too. No cinnamon sticks, I can't resist them."

"They come with the extra large pizzas. I'll hide 'em from you, in my room," Jason teased, but when he saw Jill might think he was serious he called out, as he left, "Not really, Mom."

Jill watched Jason's car disappear around the bend in her driveway. She knew she'd have to work on her thoughts about damnable Rob taking her baby boy away. She shook her head and thought of Dean. She had to ask herself, whether she had some inner work about loss to do, or what?

Jill had a little time to mulch some of her planting beds before getting ready for work. That felt good. Still, by eight o'clock she was off to a full day's work. Hard as her job was at times, she had to admit it was fulfilling. On the way to morning team meeting, she stopped by the grocery store again. It was her turn to bring the snack. She was a little indecisive about what to bring. Everyone had started to bring the same things, and there wasn't much variety. She was hungry for a banana, so she bought those, but what else? She passed by the bakery case. They had a new item, Chinese pork buns. It struck her as the thing to buy. She also remembered to pick up a good supply of diapers for her mom. That was one aisle she was not familiar with. Remembering to call them by their politically correct name of adult incontinence supplies, as they were known around hospice, she'd asked and the clerk had to direct her there.

Most everyone was already at work. Jill loved the short, informal time they had before the morning's more formal team meeting and official review of policies and patients. This earlier time was relaxed, and although everyone worked they also chatted. Jill's first question was for Kim, the chaplain.

"What did you think about the Bense funeral yesterday? And what on earth possessed the wife to plunk down that coffin lid?"

"I talked to her later," Kim said. "Mrs. Bense said she thought she saw someone there who didn't deserve to see her husband since he never bothered to come around while he was still alive. So, she just did it."

"Kim," Jill remonstrated, "Those kinds of funerals, with hardly anyone there and no one apparently even liking the deceased, just shouldn't happen."

"Oh, I don't know," Kim remarked. "Ask Donna."

"What?"

"Jill," Donna said, "Kim came back with four large checks for our indigent patient fund. Sometimes people give out of guilt."

"Don't we all know that," Dean remarked, standing at the copy machine.

Ron, Jill's nursing partner, spoke, "You know, I just remembered another funeral that was weird. Did I tell you about the Johnson twins?" he asked.

"Tell." They all clamored, since Ron always had good stories.

"These ladies were at least eighty years old. Lane saw them for me once. Remember, Lane?" He asked as he looked over toward her nursing space.

"Uh-huh, I remember. I couldn't get over how they always dressed alike. I didn't even know that identical twins used to do that all the time."

"Anyway," Ron continued, "Trudy and Judy belonged to the same church Tammy and I attend. So we went to Trudy's funeral mass. Sure enough, the deceased was dressed in a nice blue chiffon dress with pearls, and so was her twin, Judy, who sat in the front row. The poor priest was a young guy, and he looked so confused."

"That must have been trippy," Sandy, the bath aide, chimed in.

"It got worse. It seems they belonged to the Double Take organization. Many of the people attending the mass were elderly twins and dressed alike as well. Tammy and I could barely suppress our laughter. We didn't mean to, but we couldn't help it. We kept shaking, and everyone thought I must be the grandson of Trudy or something because I looked so broken up."

It was hard not to laugh, picturing that scene. Reverential chuckles, of course.

"I remember Judy," Dean said. "She felt as if half of her died with her sister. She never did get over it. She told me she pretended that Trudy had just stepped out and would be right back. That's the way she handled her grief. Sometimes those up in years approach it that way. One man told me his time was limited so he couldn't spend his remaining time in sadness. In those cases, I've realized that you can't call it denial; it's a conscious choice almost. That's the way Judy did it, and she was able to continue to live. Even when she moved down South, I received notes from her with an addendum on the bottom saying, 'Trudy says hello too, but she just went to the store so she couldn't sign.'"

This was followed by silence. The sad and the funny were sometimes so close in the human brain. Jill wanted to ask Dean about how to help Mr. Goulden with the loss of his father, but she didn't want to bring the subject up right then.

After a few moments, Dean announced, "By the way, everyone, Stuart is taking a short hiatus. He said he needs to 'reconsider his agenda.'"

"Is that because he lost the stare down?" Lane asked.

"It's not called a stare down; it's a conflict resolution strategy. A CRS," Dean insisted. "I might even call it a CRE. The E for exercise. I'll have pre-CREs and post-CREs."

"Oh my goodness," Donna said, while everyone else laughed, but in a kind way. No one would ever think of hurting Dean's feelings. He was their collective conscience. The good angel that sat on their right shoulders whenever they became too cynical. Dean was a sober presence.

"It ended on good terms. Richard and Stuart shook hands and seemed to have a more genuine rapport. Stuart will be back, and Richard was able to get in touch with some of his own issues. I'm writing the paper now. Only an 'n of one,' but it could catch on." Dean said with great confidence.

"What's the paper's title?" Donna asked.

"Tentatively, it's entitled, 'The X Factor in Small Space Therapy for Conflict Resolution.'"

"What's the X Factor?" Ron asked.

"That's what I'm working on," Dean answered. He smiled, knowing that was rather an enigmatic answer.

"It would never work with me," Sandy said.

"How do you know?" Kim asked.

"I get too itchy when I sit still."

Everyone nodded in recognition of the truth of that statement.

Kim announced during a lull, "I know everyone has been curious about my brain MRI results. Just to put your minds at ease, they found nothing, everything there was clear. Perfectly normal."

"Oh, that's a miracle," Jill said, in all seriousness. Really, though, it could be taken two ways, and that did get a chuckle out of several people in the room.

Donna asked, "That's wonderful, but since they couldn't find any problem with your brain, what are they telling you now?"

"That it's all in my head," Kim said, laughing as she said it.

***

Team meeting began in earnest after several comments about Jill's food selection. The main complaint was that the buns were too dry. So Donna went to the fridge and retrieved an extra large container of cream cheese to slather on the buns, and everyone was happy. They even liked Dean's comment about being more adventurous about the snacks. This from a man who'd brought orange slices and bran muffins every single time it was his turn to contribute.

Donna took a minute to discuss Mr. Goulden, assuring the team he was a genuine patient. She briefly alluded to the fact that the, now deceased, elder Goulden took advantage of his son.

"And here I thought my family was bad," Sandy said in a most sorrowful way.

Bill looked at his watch to let Donna know that was enough about Goulden. He apparently wanted to announce something he thought much more important.

He began in top form. "The subject this morning is accountability," he announced. "For that reason, I'm passing around our new business model. Please see the pages I've marked. This will allow us a detailed look at everyone's productivity. The consultant states that using this method could increase units seen per day, and I'm sure you workers will applaud its fairness."

Everyone reluctantly picked up a ream of paperwork from the middle of the table.

Ron made a quiet aside to Jill, "Units? Remember those other times?"

"Yes," Jill answered, "all too well."

"For instance," Bill began the review of the new idea, "An open to service counts one and one-half, revisits are ones, lab draws are one-half, let's see…bandage changes are three-fourths. We want to include all the work we do, so emotional support is one-fourth," he finished, proudly.

Lane jumped right in, "So if I do an open, change a bandage, and give emotional support, I get two and one-half. Is that a good number?"

"Lane, that's excellent math, and fast too," Donna said in amazement.

"Also," Michelle asked, "What number, are we supposed to reach, and is it the same for all disciplines?"

"Lane, dear," Bill said in his most paternalistic manner, "Look at your sample page. Bandage and support would be included in the number of one. As for other questions, please check the manual you have in front of you."

"Huh?" Sandy asked. "Then what about taking supplies out and crap?"

Bill, now becoming impatient, rattled his papers and said, "They are…"

"Not on the list. And that's something I have to do—a lot."

"Add them in. We'll make them one-halves," Bill said quickly.

Kim, who hadn't spoken thus far, now gave her list of concerns. "They have the same amount of time for planning a funeral and spiritual brokerage. Amazingly wrong. No one has included baptisms, house blessings, and spirit fests and other important services for me."

"Spirit fests?" Sandy asked, and was ignored.

Lane, trying to fill out a sample page, exclaimed, "What about patients in the western territory that I had to take over? That's a lot of extra mileage!"

Pleased he'd found one thing he'd certainly prepared for, Bill said, "Look on the last page. You'll see mileage is added at the end of the month. Anyone with excess mileage will be given points. This plan is ingenious. You see, people, this has all been worked out. Just because it's new, you may have a tendency to discount it. I'm always running uphill trying to carry everyone on my back."

A short moment of silence ensued. The staff appeared to be trying to imagine that picture.

"Bill," Donna said, "It's new, and for the workers it may, initially, seem a bit impersonal."

"My thought exactly," Dean volunteered. "We've discussed this before and concluded our patients would become numbers instead of people with real needs."

"'Units? It doesn't seem right somehow," Jill said.

"Not right?" Bill repeated, raising his voice. "Not right to increase our productivity and have happier workers? This is the kind of stonewalling I get every time I employ a progressive and enlightened idea. This topic is not up for discussion. End of matter."

"I think we need to get it all in the open, Bill. We all need to discuss it," Michelle said.

Donna agreed, "We may as well hash it all out. Then there's a better chance it will work."

Bill said, defensively, "I hired a top consultant on your behalf, staff. We paid her a good amount of money."

Finally Dr. Almerst, the usually taciturn medical director, spoke. "How much?" he asked.

Bill was now actually getting red-faced. He lowered his voice a little but didn't answer the doctor directly. "The consultant's pay and bonuses are dependent upon the meeting of our goals, and your annual raises are dependent upon it as well. You have the forms. It begins today."

"One last little question," Donna ventured. "Has this consultant had success in other hospices with this extreme, conveyer-belt method?"

Bill turned and looked at Donna, frowning. "You would think all the management would automatically support this, Donna. But apparently that's not the case. Remember, we're to be the consultant's shining example. It's a new concept. Also, it's one that should work. And I didn't hear these objections when it was explained on paper."

"My marriage works on paper," Sandy said, listlessly. She didn't appear to care about this discussion at all.

"I'm not against trying it," Lane said, "but how many points do we get for filling out all this extra paperwork?"

"Good point," Ron chimed in.

Jill flipped to the back of the manual, noting several blank pages, entitled "My Productive Day."

"None. Subject closed. Start today." Bill was through explaining.

"Okay, but how many points do we put down for the time here in team?" Ron asked.

"How many points for lectures?" Michelle queried.

"Gotten and given." Lurline said, nodding her head toward Michelle.

"Enough!" Bill exclaimed as he stood. "Start today."

"I hope you don't think I'm going to start this, Bill," Dr. Almerst said quietly.

"No. No. It's for the field workers."

"Don't they have enough to do?" Dr. Almerst asked.

"Doctor," Bill yelled, "You approved this at the manager's meeting last week."

"I did? Oh well, somehow it didn't seem as cruel when that lady was pitching it."

Bill had no immediate answer.

Unfortunately, Dean took that moment to speak up. "Bill, I see I'm included, of course. However, I need more points for family bereavement versus one-on-one. Also, there should be another point indicator for groups. We need to include our summer agape day camp for the youth. Kim helps with that too. Sir, I don't think the consultant understands what it takes to share the pain of our bereaved."

Bill, appearing that he'd totally lost control, focused on Dean. "Everyone is to try it for a while to see," adding, his voice tinged with sarcasm: "and Dean, I'm not sure any of us understand what you do."

The staff saw Dean wince after hearing that comment, and noting Dean's distress they glared at Bill. Donna reached over and patted Dean's arm. Several people got up and headed toward more refreshments. But the slightly unripe bananas and pork buns were not enticing.

There was nothing left to do but plod through the patient review…noting once again that there were entirely too many interesting *units*, who may or may not earn *points*.

***

After team, the dispirited workers retreated to their workspace, carrying their new accountability planners.

"I need my journal," Jill said.

"Just when I start a job, where I can take time to talk to my patients, I can't do it anymore," an obviously disheartened Lane commented. "Now, maybe I won't get to take my lunch time."

Ron and Jill looked toward Lane in amazement, both thinking the same thought: Lane took lunch time?

"Hard schedule today?" Jill asked Ron.

"About half and half I think. I'm not worried about making my units. But sadly, I got a call from Mr. Wedge, and his new heart medication isn't helping."

"Need any help, Ron?"

"Nah, I just like that old guy," Ron said. "He showed me how to fill out the stat sheets on all the ball players. Turns out he used to play semipro here in town for a B team back in the '50s. Do you remember him, Jill?" Ron asked.

"Remember him? Ah, not when he was a ball player," she laughed. "Did you forget that he was my patient for two months, before we changed the territory boundaries? Very nice man, with a lovely wife."

"Yeah, I like that old guy," Ron repeated.

"I see here we're supposed to do five points a day," Lurline proclaimed loudly enough for everyone to hear.

"Really? Just that much for everybody?" Michelle asked. "That's doable, especially when I note the extras."

"We should have read this further before hassling Bill. Half the stuff I do already—and don't get credit for—is in here and worth points," Lurline said, to nobody in particular.

Sandy stopped by Jill's desk before leaving. "I hope you're gonna see Mr. Dobson first," she said.

"Yes, I am. Unless I get some kind of emergency first."

"Somebody called from the house, and Dobson is now an emergency,"

"Why?" Jill asked, hurriedly packing her things up in order to leave.

"He's stuck in a doorway, and they want you out there. I can't go until the afternoon because I have to see your Joyce Sealy. You know what their house is like. Once I get there, I have to fight my way through their disgusting home just to get to her bed. Then I have to throw about three smelly animals off the bed, including her ferret, before I can even begin to bathe her."

"I'll hurry and see Dobson now, Sandy, and I know the Sealy family is messy."

"He's a first-class hoarder, and it's unsafe. You need to call the county authorities."

"Sandy," Jill began her explanation, "Michelle's involved. Remember last month the health department was called and that didn't work. They can only look at very narrow criteria. It's not bad enough out there. I have an appointment at the end of the week. Michelle has rounded up another family member, and she's been given permission to talk to her about conditions of the home, but they can't meet until next week. She'll include the idea that if it's unsafe for the workers we can't come to the house. We're working on it. Please do the best you can, meanwhile."

"I could die there, be eaten by animals and never found. That's happened, you know."

"Not to you."

"Not yet! I'm putting down two unit points for that lady. I mean it. You need to back me up on that one to Bill and Donna," Sandy added while leaving.

"Units," Ron said, speaking in a robotic voice. "I'm off to see my allotted units." That made Jill smile.

***

Michal Poe

Jill kept smiling all the way as she hurried to her first visit. Her work invigorated her. Where on earth was there a more interesting job?

Jill had opened Mr. Dobson two weeks ago. She'd seen him twice since. Each time it had been at a different address. He was a very young-looking seventy-year-old. He still had a thick shock of hair with its natural red color. Today, Jill was to go to his daughter Kate's house. Kate had been at the original meeting. Now, since Kate worked two waitress jobs, her husband, a part-time truck driver, was managing care. Or perhaps he was mismanaging it. Jill didn't know, but she was on her way to see her patient and find out.

When Jill arrived, she was told, "Bob's stuck in the bathroom doorway."

"Umm, Jerry," she said, addressing the young man who'd retreated back to the couch to watch the morning TV judge shows, "How long has he been there?"

"Well, for quite a while. I had to wait until the office opened to call. We needed somebody to tell us what to do."

Jill shook her head, amazed at how dependent people became once hospice became involved. But she only said, "I'll check."

As she approached the bathroom, she saw the patient was craning his neck around the corner to see her. "Mr. Dobson…Bob," Jill asked, "How can I help you?"

"Get me out of this damned contraption. This wheelchair is like a prison. I need to take a piss and then I need to stretch out on that couch."

"Alright," Jill said. "We'll do that."

After seeing that the metal cogs of the wheels were wedged into the wood of the doorjamb, she called Jerry over and told him he'd have to remove the bathroom door. He could act now that he had instructions, and he went to the garage to get the tools. Meanwhile she quickly washed and gloved up in the kitchen. She retrieved Dobson's urinal from a supply bag she found on the dining room table and held it while he urinated.

"I was about ready to blow!" He exclaimed. "Man, that felt good. Thanks."

Jill called, "You're welcome," over her shoulder as she went to put the urinal in a safe place until she could empty it into the toilet. Right now that would mean climbing over Dobson, which was not a possibility.

Jerry plodded back and loosened the hinges. The door was easily lifted off, and the offending doorjamb came with it. Jill then wheeled Bob back to the living room and asked Jerry to help transfer Bob to the couch.

"Me? Help?" Jerry asked almost incredulously. "Can't you nurses do that?"

"I'll show you how to move him," Jill said.

Jerry was very tentative in his movements, as if he thought his father-in-law might break, since Bob moaned more than once.

"Are you in pain?" Jill asked.

"No, I just want to get back down," Bob groaned.

After she and Jerry successfully transferred him to a comfortable position on the couch, she kindly asked Jerry to turn down the television so she could get answers to her questions. It's not that the patient couldn't hear her, but she noticed it was hard for him to concentrate. He continuously diverted his attention back to the fascinating legal case. Would the woman have to pay for the damage done to her ex-boyfriend's car? Even Jill wanted to know.

Michal Poe

She reviewed some of the important hospice policies for Jerry, since he hadn't been at the first meeting in the home. She emphasized the night line number. "See, guys, you can call day or night to get instructions and, if need be, someone can even come out here. You don't have to wait until our office opens." Then she wrote 24 HOURS in large letters on the front of Bob's folder, which, miraculously, was in the home.

She obtained vital signs from the patient and gave a few instructions regarding medications. She emptied the urinal and rinsed it out, showing Jerry which bag she'd found it in. She let Bob and Jerry know that Sandy, the bathing aide, would be by in the early afternoon.

Right before she left, Jill asked Bob, "Should I call your daughter Kate and let her know how things are?"

"Hell, she'd cuss Jerry out and I don't want to worry her."

"I'll tell her when she gets home from work," Jerry volunteered.

"Thank you, nurse, I feel great now," Bob stated. Then he added, "Turn up that TV, Jerry, you know I don't hear well."

Thus Jill earned her first "unit point" at an amazingly quick and easy first visit of her day. She called Donna to see if Michelle would phone the original daughter who had made the hospice referral. A family meeting for all involved in Dobson's care was needed—the sooner, the better. It was a large family, and Jill didn't want to be in the position of explaining the entire hospice program one-on-one to each and every household every time Bob was moved. This switching hampered meaningful communication. So far it was a new location every five days. Not a record, since families found caregiving harder in cases in which one person couldn't or wouldn't oversee the care. But it was confusing for the patient and the nurses as well. She also called Lurline, the physical therapist, who would be able to show Bob how to transfer from bed to wheelchair all by himself. He had the strength but lacked technique.

Jill wasn't upset by the son-in-law's reluctance to help. There were very few people who enjoyed physical caregiving. In the earlier days of hospice, some nurses did a lot of the lifting themselves. But since she couldn't be there twenty-four hours a day, Jill had learned to help teach others who were available.

Jill thought of Valerie, an excellent hospice nurse with whom Jill had worked for almost six months, before Valerie went off to a teaching job. This was after Bill came on board as manager. She was into all the alternative medicines and was a very vigorous and strong woman. She claimed it was her daily regimen of herbs and such, but actually it was steroids. Although she didn't last long in the home-health field, the patients and the staff loved her. Legend said she'd been able to lift and move even the heaviest of patients without caring anything about the fulcrum point.

***

Her second patient was an initial visit to open Harry McCarthy to hospice services. His wife, Linda, had provided most of the information Jill had with her in a folder. He and his wife were both eighty-two years old. Up to this point, they'd been very independent. It looked like a good care situation, and both the McCarthys were happy about the idea of a "holistic approach with hospice." Jill headed toward the couple's communal home. She had been to this small enclave at the edge of her territory more than once. It was always an interesting place to visit. The man at the entrance gate recognized her and waved her through. It was a chilly morning, and Jill was glad she was warmly dressed.

Harry had asked that they meet in the day room, explaining that their own bedroom suite was very small. The day room was spacious and populated. They found a quiet corner and Jill began her explanations and paperwork.

Since she was a nurse and was used to seeing naked bodies, it didn't concern her that she was the only one in the room who was dressed. The Nature's Way with Sunshine Nudist Colony was one of the oldest in the state. It was historical. The buildings were monumental. Except for noticing that the day room was kept very warm (she had to concede she was probably overdressed), she was comfortable with the environment.

"'Healthy living,' that's Harry's motto," Linda offered. "He's the original health nut. He once met Jack Lalanne, you know."

"That's true," Harry said. "I made up my own exercise routine too." He raised his arms for emphasis. "Even when I was in the army, I ate no red meat. Got razzed plenty about that."

"He was crushed, weren't you, Harry? To find out you were so sick." She turned toward Jill. "It was a shock." She paused a moment. "He was a shy guy when I met him, decent man, never drank…" Linda's eyes were noticeably misting up.

"I blame myself," Harry interrupted. It was obvious that he'd become very concerned when he saw his wife become emotional. "I admit it, I used to smoke. Not for long, but long enough for this damn lung cancer thing to get going, I guess."

"Let's see," Jill said, looking at her notes. "You smoked for three years, and quit over sixty years ago?"

"Yup, I'll be eighty-three soon."

Linda, now smiling, said, "I think he thought he'd live forever."

"Not forever," Harry interjected, "But I wanted to die in good shape." They both laughed uproariously. These convivial sounds attracted several others over to the corner. Jill had quite an audience as she, with the McCarthys' permission, continued with her full assessment after most of the paper signing.

When Jill had explained the Do Not Resuscitate form in detail, as she was mandated to do, Harry looked shocked. He began to wave his hands around. Jill wasn't sure what his reaction was going to be, but she sighed with relief at his explanation.

"For God's sake, why would anyone want to be brought back? I think it would be hard enough to die once."

Jill was pleased, as she never knew what the patient would have to say on the matter. Harry quickly signed the paperwork.

"One more question, Jill."

"Yes."

"If I'm in a lot of pain or something, do you guys help me check out of the hotel, so to speak?"

Linda gave a little gasp. "Harry," she said sternly. "You shouldn't even ask such a thing. They're going to think you're crazy or suicidal or something."

Michal Poe

Jill knew it would be important how she answered this question. She had a big audience, and she needed to let Harry know what the hospice parameters were. She needed to normalize his question too.

"Harry, I get that same question a lot. No one knows how things are going to go, and people want options. But you know, we don't help things along. Our goal is comfort. Comfort is our main concern. That's what we work on. That's what people appreciate the most too."

Harry nodded. "See, Linda, she doesn't think I'm crazy." Harry looked right into Linda's eyes. "Honey, you know I plan on living right up to the time I die."

"But Harry…"

"It's like she said, I just want to know my options."

Linda seemed satisfied with the exchange. Jill knew this type of honesty was important for all three of them.

The other people near her all appeared to be listening closely and seemed very curious about hospice. However, they were polite and didn't interrupt with their own questions or stories. Harry told them he'd leave all the brochures out so they could look at them later in case they ever needed such a service.

No one there in the day room was under sixty years old. Everyone sat on little hand towels they each carried around. When they got up to walk away, Jill noticed terry cloth imprints on all their bottoms. It struck her as cute, somehow. Jill saw beauty in the human form. One of the nurses from her team, and a few from the other team, had made disparaging remarks about the lack of nice figures and physiques of the patrons there. Jill felt that nurses, of all people, should know bodies were marvelous, amazing things, so wondrously made. They had bought into the same Madison Avenue sell that unless you were perfect, your body didn't count. She'd never found anyone with the perfect body, according to their own self-assessment. She, although slim, had noticed her body heading south. Maybe it was looking for sunshine.

With the assessment complete, Linda was continuing with her "love that guy" stories. "Jill, do you know he gave up driving on his own? Nobody had to come and take his license away."

"That's unusual, and very commendable."

"I wanted to quit before I hurt somebody," Harry offered. He smiled as he shifted in his chair.

Linda continued, "He's made me a book, too, with all the important information in it. Then he arranged for his mother's care in a wonderful facility."

Jill was surprised but tried not to show it. She asked Harry, "Your mother is still alive?"

"She'll be one hundred on Friday. She's amazing. I guess that's another reason I thought I'd live longer. If you come Friday, you can share her carrot cake. They're bringing her out here. I'm the only child she has left." He spoke loudly and announced to all in the area, "Hey, everybody here, remember Effie's birthday is Friday in this room, at noon. No presents though, please."

Linda stood up as she continued with her praise but left her little towel on the chair. "He's left all the information for next year's income taxes. We still pay. Investments, you know. And Harry and I have an estate plan. The annuity will help rebuild some of this wonderful facility's lost beauty. Maybe that will get more young people interested in health," Linda proudly declared.

"Vitamins." Harry proclaimed. "I invested in companies when it was a new idea. Vitamin D is going through the roof now. People don't want to get things natural. It's supplements all the way. We sell to other countries now, too. Jill, have you heard of McCarthy Vit-a-Health?"

"No," Jill admitted, "I haven't."

"Good," Harry said. "We keep a low profile."

Jill was enjoying her visit. Linda sat down again, after rearranging her towel and pulling her chair closer so she could watch Jill take the vital signs and write the numbers on a graph sheet she had with her. Harry let Jill know that the only current problem he was experiencing was his bowels. He'd tried all the regimens to "get things going" that had worked in the past. He tried to reach under the chair to get something. Linda retrieved it for him.

"See," he said, "I wanted to show you something. I bought this special squat stool device. You put it under your feet when you are on the toilet. But it's too tall."

Jill looked at it, but couldn't exactly figure out how it would work on somebody in Harry's weakened condition. Certainly he was now too frail to climb up on such an item. Harry acquiesced that all those things were now unsuccessful. He was pleased to hear Jill knew most all of them, and even a few more. Jill could see he stayed hydrated. His fatigue, causing inactivity, was new to him and the probable cause of his sluggish intestinal condition. One of the other members on the periphery of the group, Ira, appeared to be listening closely and apparently had an idea. He left and came back with a little portable standing foot cycle for Harry.

"Now," Ira said, "you'll move your lower half and get things really moving."

Harry and Linda were very pleased. Jill thought it might work as well. Linda put it under his feet, and Harry started pumping away while still sitting in his chair. "Get the name of this contraption," he said to his wife. "If this works we'll manufacture them. A 'bowelcycle.'"

"Oh, Harry," Linda remonstrated.

"A 'poop processor,'" Ira said.

"It's a state of the art 'excrement extractor,'" another member chimed in.

Jill laughed, saying, "I can tell this whole meeting is at its *end*, so I'll *run* on out of here. Thanks for everything. Harry, Linda, I'll see you Friday."

"Yeah, nurse, time for you to *bow-el out*," one of the men shouted out, to everyone's delight.

As she left she heard other members trying out names, puns, and cute bathroom jokes the conversation brought to mind. They were in some kind of wonderful word world she'd seen bright people enter. Tripping through their vast store of linguistics, they sometimes found it hard to get out. It was simply delightful to hear, on the one hand, yet a little scary for Jill. She'd already noticed that tendency in herself.

Back in her Jeep, she took a minute to write a note on Harry's chart, "Dress lightly, keeps very warm in there." She had actually worked up a sweat and had to turn on the air conditioner.

***

Jill was trying to enjoy her healthy lunch. She munched on her raw veggies and managed to get down her baba ganoush. During the whole meal, she was anticipating that night's pizza. She put in a call to Jason. He could take cell-phone calls during his lunch hour at school. Now that Stina was in family day care, he didn't go home for lunch. Jill knew that was better for him, although he never complained about having to go home to help his grandmother with her lunch when he did do it for her.

"I told Sherrice, dinner sometime between six and seven, right?" he asked.

"That will be wonderful," Jill answered.

A call from Sandy beeped through, so she cut her call short and switched over.

Sandy was in a dither. "Jill, I told you so," Sandy yelled. Before Jill could answer she rattled on. "Now they got a new animal. I'm telling you, Sealy brought home a snake! He didn't know snakes and ferrets were like mortal enemies. You should see this place. You know those zillion stacks of newspapers Joyce was saving for who knows what? Looks like a ticker tape parade in there. Nobody can find Mr. Slithers now, and Foxy the ferret is missing too. I can't do it, Jill. You know how I want things nice for her, and I can't do it."

Jill could tell Sandy was on the brink of tears. "Okay, Sandy," she said. "Don't worry about it today. I'll see the Sealys and check it out. I can give the bath if she needs one. You calm yourself and go on to the next patient. We'll work it out. I'll let you know how things go."

Sandy settled down a little with Jill's assurance that she'd be backed up. Jill also told Sandy she remembered something the health department had said. "The law says that in that part of the city only three animals are allowed per household. Maybe I could talk to Joyce about that."

"That's if all the animals are still alive!" Sandy exclaimed.

Jill acknowledged that possibility. "So true."

After hanging up with Sandy, she reviewed where she could get some help for a co-visit. She knew she needed some help. Michelle, the social worker, was the obvious choice, but Jill knew she was at a conference until three so she wouldn't be available.

Jill made a call to Ron, and he agreed to meet her at the Sealys' if she would see Chase Miller for him. He explained that Chase might not need that visit today, but Ron wasn't sure, as he hadn't called the family yet. Jill had hesitated, just for a moment, about the patient exchange. Chase was only twenty-two years old, with a reported problematic family, and she knew it would be a hard visit, but feasible.

She asked Ron to bring trash bags with him and possibly the animal cage from the supply closet. Ron didn't ask why. They worked too well together to waste time asking why.

It was beginning to look like her day might entail some overtime, since she had to meet Michelle for a first visit at three. That visit to open the patient to hospice services was expected to be a difficult one. Both Lane and someone from the other team had tried to open this prospective patient, and she'd sent them away. The patient's doctor was frantic. He knew how much help hospice could be. Adele Fromm was a stickler for detail, and her husband, the doctor had told them, behaved stoically, but he could use the help just as much.

Before she hung up, and still curious, she asked Ron what he'd changed around on his schedule. Ron admitted he was going to an early ball game.

"Oh, Ron, I didn't know. When you take time off, you usually tell me ahead of time."

"I'm not taking time off," Ron clarified, "I'm taking Wedge to one of those great afternoon ballgames, the first of a double header. Their helper couldn't do it, so I agreed. Wedge has box seats."

"On company time?"

"It's a visit, Jill. The first hour of the game will be considered a visit. I talked to Donna, and she talked to the Wedges. It's arranged."

"Who talked to Bill?"

"That's another matter. Maybe, to be fair, I'll subtract one-half a unit point. You know the satisfaction factor."

Jill laughed, "Well, in that case, if it's subjective, I'd have to reconsider my last visit. That was very pleasant. See you at the Sealys' at one?"

"Roger," Ron assured her in his robotic voice from earlier.

If she was being perfectly honest, Jill didn't want to go into the Sealys' house alone because she was afraid of snakes. She knew it was a cliché, and she fought against it. She loved that there were garden snakes in and around her property. They were so useful. Because of her allergies, she couldn't have cats at her place, and the snakes kept the vermin in check. Her fear of snakes began that the day of the "fence incident," as C.J. called it. He'd witnessed the scene and still laughed uproariously every time he told it. Jill had been picking cucumbers in her garden, her first summer there. She reached in and found a nice big, cool one, and pulled it out to put in her basket. It was then that she realized she had grasped and was now looking straight into the face of a very large bull snake. C.J. said she cleared the six-foot fence with room to spare.

Jill - Hospice Nurse, Book Two: Last Exit

***

Now at the Sealys' address, Jill waited outside the home in her car for Ron. From her vantage point, the house looked rather neat. That was one reason the health department couldn't bring in the code people. But inside, the house was entirely another matter. Dangers lurked within.

Jill was able to finish all her morning reports on her laptop. It was a pleasant day. The air was fresh, and Jill made sure she let a little sunshine hit her skin. Ron arrived on his motorcycle. He appeared to be in an exceptionally good mood. He was already wearing his ball cap.

He and Jill entered the home very cautiously. It looked like the same mess it had always been, except the hallway to the bedroom was more paper strewn. Mr. and Mrs. Sealy were friendly. Mr. Sealy always looked like an unmade bed himself, as Sandy had so colorfully depicted him. Mrs. Sealy, or Joyce, as she insisted on being called, welcomed them graciously.

"Hello there, everybody. Sorry about the mess," Joyce said.

Jill realized that Joyce must have repeated that line about one hundred times in the two months Jill had been her nurse. Jill could never figure out which of the couple was the worst hoarder. She could see that they both contributed.

"Hey," Mr. Sealy bellowed, "Thought you nurses would have that little social worker with you, after the way Sandy ran outta here." He laughed. "Sure hope we didn't hurt her feelings."

Ron, with a trash sack in hand, had stayed in sight but was still in the hallway. At this point he spoke, "Hello there. Say Len, listen, these shredded papers are a slipping hazard here in the hallway. Since they're ruined anyway, may I remove them?"

"Oh yeah," Len answered. "They're trash now."

Ron put on his rubber gloves and went to work. It would be a wide hallway with everything removed. Jill then noticed a very small dog that was eating out of a cereal bowl on Joyce's bedside table. Jill wondered how it had gotten up there.

Noticing Jill staring at the dog, Len said, "Oh, let me get Poochie out of your way." He unceremoniously dumped everything, including the dog, onto the floor.

Jill used her hand gel and did a quick visit summary for her records. Ron continued with a second and then a third bag on his trash removal. He was now infringing upon the first corner of the sickroom.

Jill stopped him by saying, "Ron could you come over here? Let's talk about things with the family."

Jill knew that removing more than what patients allowed from their homes, no matter how unsafe or unsettling the messes were for the staff, was very upsetting for the patients. The health department had recently given a lecture at the hospice office. Dean had arranged it, since this subject fell under the broad sweep of loss. The health officer had said that removing even a bottle cap might seem as wrenching to them as losing one's mother's heirloom ring. It was a good lecture. Jill now saw this extreme condition as a type of psychological problem and therefore part of her patient's body. It needed to be handled with care. But even with care, it must be handled.

Jill patiently explained the safety rules under the auspices of hospice. Several times, she let them know that everything was their choice, but she said the animals needed to be more confined and a clear path to the patient from the front door and around the patient's bedside were the standard rules for service in the home. Both Len and Joyce were quiet for a bit.

Finally, Len said, "You know, when I brought that snake home, I didn't realize Joyce hated snakes. Can you imagine that? So if we find it, I'll take it back or let it loose or something. I hope it didn't kill Foxy, though. They were really going at it."

Joyce, more serious than Jill had ever heard her, said to her husband, "I don't want to go to a nursing home; could we please do a little on the house?"

Jill hadn't mentioned a nursing home; she would never threaten that. It sometimes happened that the family couldn't care for the patient in the home. However, Jill considered it cruel to mention it in any other way except as an alternate care choice. Even then, she included it only at times when she was reviewing all the patient's viable options.

Len looked down at his hands. He asked, "Just a clear pathway?"

"With stuff on the sides arranged so as to not fall over on anyone. Then the wall sockets need to be cleared by at least twelve inches," Ron added. Seeing Len was about to capitulate, he sealed the deal by saying, "And since I've got the time, I'll help you today."

"We'll do it!" Len exclaimed hurriedly, as if he knew if he thought about it he couldn't have done it.

Joyce looked at her husband. "Come here, you big baby, and give me a hug." Len lumbered over, stepping on the cereal bowl but missing the dog. He leaned down, gave his wife a hug, then followed Ron out the bedroom door. Jill heard Ron discussing the need to start at the front door and just follow through. Fortunately, Ron had brought an extra large box of leaf bags. Jill used the opportunity to give Joyce a nice warm bed bath. After thirty minutes, she was all finished, and Ron appeared at the bedroom door with the snake around his neck. He didn't enter, knowing Joyce hated snakes.

"Look! Guess where we found Mr. Slithers?" Ron asked. But it was just a rhetorical question, as he quickly added, "He and Foxy were holed up in a corner sleeping together, just like old friends. See?" He held up Foxy, who was nestled in his arms. "No bite marks on either of them."

Both Joyce and Jill winced.

"Joyce," Ron continued, "Your husband says I can take the snake home. That way you won't have to bother with it. I have a cage with me, but he wanted me to check with you first."

"Oh, take it away, please, take it away," Joyce pleaded.

Jill was thinking the same thought. She wondered how Ron was going to report this gift on their new gift acceptance form. Lurline, the physical therapist, had recently filled one out. She'd put down that she'd been given—and ate—an apple at a patient's home. Management didn't think that was funny.

Ron washed his hands and removed his protective clothing. Then, outside the home, he used a prodigious amount of hand sanitizer before and after hooking the cage back onto the back of his motorcycle, saying, "Jill, I'll have to take Mr. Slithers home before the game. So I guess that puts you in charge of waste removal."

Ron had taken all seven of the filled trash bags and thrown them in the back of Jill's Jeep.

"Sorry, I don't have room on my cycle," he joked, adding a reminder: "You need to drop these by the big office trash can. I remember that health lady said that if you don't totally remove things from the home, some people pull everything out of their trash and replace it back where it was."

"Good thinking. Do you think Tammy will like the snake?"

"My wife loves animals and my son will really like it. He's into reptiles."

"How old is Jake now?"

"Seven."

"I remember Jason was into reptiles and dinosaurs at that age too. Boys," Jill said. "Boys," she repeated. She was thinking now that Jason was soon becoming a man. Now that was a scary thought. Scarier than snakes for her.

Jill used her speaker phone to let Michelle, the social worker, know she'd set the time at Adele Fromm's for the first visit and open to services (hopefully) at three-fifteen, so they could both be on time. Adele's folder had indicated that she was strict about punctuality. Jill always thought it best to accommodate scheduled appointment times as closely as possible, especially on the first visit.

When Jill called Ron's patient, Chase, his mother let Jill know that Chase was very tired and would probably sleep all day. She asked if the visit could wait for the regular nurse on Wednesday or Thursday. Jill checked to see if Chase was having any medical problems, other than the usual status. He seemed stable from the phone report, so she let them know she wouldn't make the visit this day. This suited Jill's schedule just fine. She left Ron a message on his work cell phone and Donna's phone as well.

Now she would have time to drop by and pick up some supplies and a few pieces of equipment from a recent widow. The woman had left her a message that she was getting depressed looking at all that surrounded her: the raised toilet seat, the tub bench, the walker, and even all the cans of nutrition drinks and clothes from her late husband. She added that she had no way to get it out to give it away somewhere and asked if Jill could pick the articles up.

Ordinarily, Jill would have arranged for a volunteer, but she needed some closure on this case anyway. It would be a good little bereavement visit. She'd bring by literature and try to talk the widow into attending that recent loss group that Dean Cornell had started. He was trying to move the bereaved along a continuum and had separated them into "recent loss" and "long-term loss" groups. He wasn't sure how that would go, because he couldn't set a time limit in months or years. He explained there was one man who wanted the long-term group after two months. Another member insisted she stay with the newly widowed, as she'd only been a widow for eighteen months. Dean clarified the point by saying it's not the amount of time passed, but whether the emotional work has been accomplished.

Jill planned on taking the things she picked up at this visit to the thrift shop that the volunteers ran for Community Hospice. Jill liked going to that store and looking through things to see what was new. The workers and staff got a ten percent discount. Her only concern at the shop would be running into a lot of the family members who'd been recent customers of hers. They always wanted to stop and chat. Jill could understand why, but still, it could be very time consuming. She figured that today, she'd take the chance.

The picking up of these used supplies would count as a one-half visit, putting Jill at her mark. Oh, she noticed, even over her mark. She took the time to fill out her My Productive Day sheet. She also wrote, for a few minutes, in her journal. Under the topic *Letting Go*, she didn't get very far. She couldn't think of much to write.

***

The pick up and drop off went smoothly. The widow, Galena, had everything ready for Jill. It was quite a bit of stuff. When Jill mentioned the groups, she agreed to try it once.

"At least three times, Galena," Jill urged. "You need that to get a feel for the group."

"I guess I could try that. You know, none of my friends, family, or even acquaintances want to talk about...his death."

"No one knows how to sympathize anymore," Jill lamented.

"It's lonely."

"It's a strange place to be, huh?" Jill empathized.

Galena nodded, and they stood quietly for a minute. Then Galena shrugged and said, "Uh-huh."

Before they started taking the bags of clothes and the equipment out to her Jeep so Jill could take them to the thrift shop, Galena pulled out a very old pipe stem that had been stuffed down inside her bra. Jill didn't comment.

"I carry this around. I want to give it up, but I can't," Galena said, sadly.

"What is it? And what does it mean to you?"

"He used to smoke a pipe. He saved this; I don't know why. When I found it, I had to have it on me. Do you think I should see a psychiatrist or something?" she asked, as she tucked the item back in her bra.

"It's called a talisman, and many people carry around something that reminds them of their loved one. It helps them feel a connection. Sometimes it's needed."

"So it's not crazy?" Galena insisted.

"I don't think so, but you know I would mention that in that widow's group you're going to next week. I think you'll be surprised to find out that most everybody has something similar."

Galena looked relieved. "I like the old pipe tobacco smell," she said. "It reminds me of him."

Jill waited a moment, before she reached out her hand in a supportive gesture. Galena took Jill's hand and then hugged her.

"See," she said, "After I hugged one of my sisters, she told me I should fix that underwire in my bra. So I couldn't even tell her about the pipe thing. I feel better now, thanks."

Jill left after her short and productive visit.

She had to cram the articles she was taking in for Galena in front of the trash already in her Jeep. The walker was wedged into the front passenger seat. She had to pass on the portable commode. Understandably, no one ever wanted a used one of those.

She dropped things by the thrift shop. She asked and got permission to use their large trash container. They were a little disappointed, though, to find that seven of the bags Jill had were trash. One of the workers wanted to go through them to see if there was anything valuable. Jill had to talk them out of it, assuring them it had already been sorted and things were so bad that they shouldn't even pull out the newspapers for recycling as most were soiled. That put a stop to their curiosity. Jill lost the urge to shop because the store was filled with customers. This was a good thing, because it meant more money for the hospice indigent fund.

She settled back in the driver's seat of her Jeep. She had time now to get an iced tea at the corner drive-through and still meet Michelle at ten minutes after three. It always felt good to be on time.

***

They talked as they walked up to the door to see the supposedly difficult person they were to sign on, Adele Fromm. Michelle told Jill that she'd enjoyed her education class and said she was really feeling great.

"Good," Jill said. "Remember, this case may be hard."

"Did anybody say why?"

"Only that after a short visit, the patient would dismiss the worker saying, 'You won't do. Good day.' Lane said she felt as if she'd been put on a timeout bench more than once during her short try."

"I like that. She doesn't waste anyone's time. Gets to the point," Michelle said.

A tall, thin man answered the door. He introduced himself as Mr. Frank Fromm, Adele's husband. Jill and Michelle handed him their business cards. He escorted them to a small foyer and said, "Wait here, please." They heard whispered talk and scraping of chairs. Then Mr. Fromm called out, "Ladies, please enter through the vestibule and turn right."

Intrigued, Michelle and Jill followed the directions. There they saw the Fromms sitting in straight-backed chairs behind a library table that was up one step from where two chairs were arranged for Jill and Michelle. They noted the rooms were sparsely furnished. It was very shaker-like in style—all wood and no fussiness. Adele had a turban on. It appeared she'd recently taken another chemotherapy. Jill knew that it had failed. The patient was very thin but sat ramrod straight. Adele had a folder in front of her and two pens. One was red; the other was black.

"Please sit," Frank said. "This is my wife, Adele. Adele dear," he said in a formal way, "this is…" He read their business cards, "Jill Wheaten, RN, and Michelle Grant, MSW."

Adele spoke up. "My husband and I like to interview our prospective hospice workers. I'm wondering, have you two experience in home care?"

Michelle, trying to be proper and well-prepared, said, "We have a job description here. Our work records including experience, are usually kept at the office."

"Excuse me, young lady," Adele quipped, "I don't think I called on you specifically."

Feeling a little confused, Michelle asked, "What?"

"I will call your name when it's your turn to speak."

"Adele," Jill said, "I believe Donna went over all these specifics when she talked to you on the phone, just yesterday."

"Excuse me, young lady," Adele addressed Jill, "I don't think I called your name either."

Michelle and Jill looked at one another. Immediately they both knew what to do. They would play along with Adele. Since they had figured out Adele's *modus operandi*, neither of them said a word and waited for Adele to instruct.

"There, that's better," Adele said. "Now, Michelle, your résumé and experience?"

"Thank you, Ma'am," Michelle said. "Here's the résumé." She reached up and placed it on the table. And my experience is available at the hospice office."

"And Michelle," Adele queried, "just how would I obtain that?"

"Call Donna, the office manager, who'd be glad to mail or fax you a copy."

"Excellent. And you, Jill?"

"Yes, Mrs. Fromm, Adele. My résumé," she said as she too laid hers on the table. "And Donna would be happy to get you a copy of my experience. Or, I could bring it out next time."

"Wonderful! Now that wasn't so hard, was it? Would either of you like a snack? Frank," she added, before either Jill or Michelle could answer, "get these ladies a snack, please."

"Yes, dear," Frank said. He left the room after carefully getting up and scooting his chair back into its very specific place.

"Jill," Adele continued, "what is your role?"

"I'm here to check on your general health, take vital signs, and instruct as needed. I'll be informing your doctor of any changes and any concerns you or your family have."

"How often will you be coming by, Jill?"

"As often as you need me, but at least once a week."

"Fantastic!" Adele exclaimed. "Michelle, your role?"

"My role will be to provide emotional support and liaison for you and your family. That will be on an as-needed basis. I can also help your family with resources and long-term follow-up."

"Wonderful. Just wonderful. Good work. It seems they finally sent a team that listens."

Frank had returned with two small separate plates. He went over to Jill's chair and lifted up an attached tray table. He did the same with Michelle's. He set up their plates on the little space. He laid down a napkin, a small glass of milk, and two graham crackers with peanut butter in between. Jill half expected him to tuck the napkin under her chin. He then returned to his place but stood behind his chair. Michelle raised her hand slightly (not wanting to speak out of order).

"Yes, Michelle?" Adele said.

"Should we eat now?"

"Certainly, dear, you may. I'll go get undressed in my bedroom, and Jill, you come on in when you are through. That's after you wash your hands, of course. Michelle, would you kindly stay here and talk to Frank? He may have some concerns about which he feels too shy to voice in front of me." She turned on a beaming smile. "This is lovely, just lovely, ladies. This will work out splendidly."

She held her arm out, reaching for her husband's hand. "Frank?"

Frank took her arm and helped her up. He guided her from behind as they slowly headed toward Adele's bedroom. Partway there he turned his head toward Michelle and Jill and said, very quietly, "Thank you, thank you."

The rest of the visit went quickly enough. Jill and Michelle were careful to follow Adele's lead, and once in the groove it didn't seem difficult at all. Adele needed a lot of help, and Jill had come none too soon. Several medications were decided upon, and others were to be refilled. A few pieces of equipment that Adele agreed upon were ordered, and a lot of instruction was given to Frank. He had talked with Michelle for some time and appeared more comfortable with help for his wife. Jill noted that during the whole visit, Adele never relaxed and kept herself stiff and straight, no matter what position she was in. It was just her way, because there was nothing wrong with her posture, otherwise.

Jill and Michelle left, after being given permission from Adele to "take their leave" at four-thirty. Frank stood by the door and watched them depart. They'd reassured him that the nurse would be back in a few days. He had the night numbers to call, and Michelle was going to send him some of the literature she thought would be helpful for him and his wife. After they'd left the house, Jill and Michelle didn't stand on the sidewalk and talk, because they knew that would upset Adele, should she notice. They really felt like they had her number. They took to their respective vehicles to drive back to the office for the day's wrap-up.

Once back in her Jeep, Jill received a cell phone call almost immediately.

"Guess what Adele Fromm did for a living?" Michelle asked.

"I'll guess, but whatever it was I know she was good at it. That woman knows how to manage. Let's see…somewhere where order was important. Police chief?" Jill ventured.

"Two more guesses."

"Protocol secretary for the governor?"

"Good one. One more."

"Civil engineer in charge of bridge loads?"

"Okay three good guesses, but you missed the obvious one."

"Which is?"

Michal Poe

"Kindergarten teacher."

***

Jill was shocked to find Ron already back at the office. He, Dean, and Donna were hunched over his desk area. She and Michelle headed right over to see what was going on. Donna saw them and cried out, "Wait, Ron, don't start it yet. Jill and Michelle are here."

Jill noticed Ron had his mini-cam, and he put the little four-inch window on freeze frame.

Ron explained. "I went to the game and brought my camera to record what I could for my brother. He went to college with the pitcher on our team. It's a good thing I brought along all of Wedge's paperwork. Well, you'll see. Shush now, okay? I have to see what I've got."

He started the film. It showed a box seat, some shuffling, and confusion when getting the wheelchair in the best position. Then Ron had turned the camera around to face himself for a moment, then was apparently filming and sitting behind Mr. and Mrs. Wedge. Jill could see the ball field, although not that clearly. The scoreboard was visible though.

Ron fast-forwarded quite a bit. "Let's see, here's part of it, I think. Well the audio is good. After the fifth inning, the score was three to nothing; let's see what's here."

Ron's voice, from the mini-cam, could be heard now. "The fifth inning, and a no-hitter for our pitcher. What are the odds?"

Mitch Wedge checked his stat sheet, "For this guy, about six thousand to one."

Toni Wedge ignored the guys' talk and reached over, taking something from Mitch's hand. "I'm finishing your hot dog, since you left most of it. You're not supposed to eat those things anyway. It's not healthy."

"You're right," Mitch said. "I'd rather let a beer kill me."

"Fat chance," Toni said. "Chug down your sports drink."

Mitch turned around to face the camera. Speaking to Ron, he said, "I thought beer was the official sports drink."

Toni laughed, drowning out the announcer, "Ha ha, you wish. Oh look, another strikeout!"

"Really?" Mitch said. "Darn, I missed it. I'm loving this game."

"I'm so glad we're here," Toni agreed.

"Here, honey, you keep the stats. I'm gonna pay attention this next inning and just watch."

"Okay, sweetie," Toni said, taking the sheets off his lap. "You watch, and the hell with the stats."

"Hell?" Mitch asked.

Toni crossed herself, in jest. "Heck," she amended, and they both laughed.

At this point, there in the office, Ron fast-forwarded the camera again, "Here's the place I need to see," he said.

Now it appeared that Ron had set the camera on a chair, propping it up. They could see a team pennant stuck in the arm of Mitch's wheelchair. Jill could hear Ron's cell phone ring and saw him taking the call over on the side.

The whole stadium began to go wild. You could barely hear the announcer say, "This could be a record game, still a no-hitter!" Mitch was excited and cheering with his wife; it almost appeared that he was about to jump up out of his wheelchair. Then, with Ron still talking on the phone, one hand over his other ear and his back to the Wedges, Mitch winced and clutched his chest.

Michal Poe

Toni noticed. "Honey, do you need Ron? Whatever you think. Honey?"

"I think I'm having the time of my life. Thank you, Darling." He reached out and grabbed his wife's hand. With a sincere look on his face, Mitch Wedge slumped over.

The noise was continuous, Mrs. Wedge was screaming, and the announcer was yelling, "Strikeout!" It took a little while for Ron to notice what had happened to Mitch. Then he rushed over. They could see Ron checking things and then calling on his cell phone while Toni sobbed against the arm of Mitch's chair. With the camera still running and the crowd cheering, they heard the sirens from an ambulance and then saw security personnel arriving. Ron had pulled out the Do Not Resuscitate form and was showing it to the ambulance driver and others while pointing and gesticulating. In the background, the loud crack of a bat was heard. The crowd went silent for a moment.

The announcer said, "That could…" The sound was lost, and at this point the camera field went blank.

It was very quiet now in the hospice office. Finally Michelle said, in a very subdued manner, "It's good you brought his DNR form, Ron."

After a few seconds longer, Donna went to Ron and put her arms around his shoulder. Ron looked at her and smiled in recognition of her gesture.

Then Donna asked. "I'm sorry, but I need to know, Ron. How did the game end?"

"It was a no-hitter for Mitch. They only got that run in at the last minute. I heard about it on the radio driving back here. Toni was pretty calm after the initial shock. She even told me she thought it was a good death."

"That memory will help Mrs. Wedge in her grief. So fortunate for her to know he was happy when he died, so auspicious," Dean said solemnly.

There was nothing else to be said. Everyone went to their areas and simply packed up to go home, dropping by their My Productive Day sheets on Donna's desk on the way out.

Jill wrote her usual entry in her journal. True, Mitch was now Ron's patient, not hers, but he had been hers for the first few months he was on hospice, and she needed to write her impressions.

Mitch. The Good Sport.
All American, All the way.
Big League guy. Stayed in line and
Played the game, rain or shine.

***

Jill didn't pick up any of her messages on the drive home. She did stop by and order the pizzas, before she picked up her mother. If Fern noticed Jill's quietness, she didn't comment upon it. Jill went back and got the pizzas on the way home. She only ran in for one minute but was very worried about leaving her mother alone in the car, even though Stina was in plain sight through the restaurant's glass door. Her mom could no longer figure out how to undo her seat belt, but you never knew. Jill had learned that the hard way.

After she got home, she wanted to take a run but didn't have the time. She made her mother comfortable by sitting her in a patio chair. She moved some yard equipment around in case she had a spare moment in the morning to do some farm work. Then she arranged the salad for dinner and helped her mom into the living room, turning on the TV so she'd be occupied while Jill got ready for her company. Her mother still seemed to enjoy the evening news programs, which Jill didn't understand as they depressed the heck out of her. She wasn't sure what Stina took in from the television but noted her mom didn't seem to have nightmares or anything, so it was still a good and viable distraction. It gave Jill a little time.

    She took a quick shower, pinned her hair up on top of her head, applied some mascara and lip gloss, and waited for her boyfriend.

    Bennett, and then Jason with his girlfriend, Sherrice, arrived about the same time. Jill put on the new swing CD and a smile on her face and then served dinner. She ate her salad, but not much. She didn't have much of an appetite. Between Ron's fiasco and worrying about what Bennett wanted to talk about, she felt beat.

    The conversation at dinner had been light and harmless. Jason was about finished feeding Stina the rest of her pizza, and Bennett and Sherrice had already left the table. Bennett was trying to show Sherrice the basics of swing dancing. Jill went to the kitchen to get dessert. The frozen brownies she'd put in the oven earlier had burned on the bottom. As she was trying to salvage the good parts and throw them on top of some vanilla ice cream to make some kind of dessert, she started crying. The second night in a row, and she knew it wasn't hormones. She honestly was feeling sorry for herself. Not only was that not a very good feeling in general, it was a rather foreign feeling for Jill. She'd felt sorry for herself at other times in her life. She certainly knew she'd been thrown some curves, but she never allowed things to come to the surface so often as she had of late. She washed her face at the kitchen sink. The tears and the makeup were erased, but her eyes were still red.

Jason came into the room. He sensed her mood. "What's wrong, Mom?" he asked.

Jill sat down at the little kitchen table. "Jason, this is not the time nor the place, but I think I've been feeling blue because it seems you're growing up and I'm losing you."

"Losing me?"

"You know—you're about to start your life. Mom is declining. I'll be left alone."

"Mom, I won't say that's ridiculous, but it is. This reminds me of Squeekers, though."

"Squeekers?"

"Remember that cat you got after the divorce, and we lived in that little apartment for a while? No pets allowed. You brought home that short-haired cat, Squeekers?"

"I remember."

"Aside from your allergies, it was used to being an outdoor cat, and it kept escaping out the front door."

"That's true. It seemed I spent hours each evening calling for Squeekers." It sounded so funny, Jill had to smile.

"Remember what you told me when we finally found another home for him?"

"No."

"You said, 'It's not wise to keep trying to hold on to what you can't keep.'"

Jill thought for a minute. "I did say that."

"Not that you're losing me, Mom, but I understand. Sherrice said her dad is going through this too. He wants to direct her every move these days. She thinks that's why he's so interested in me. Like he thinks maybe he can give me some advice, since his daughter won't take any from him."

Jill sat in amazement. Her theory about the kid getting the best of both of his parents went out the window. It was more like when she'd mixed the hazelnut and mocha coffee creamers and ended up with a new, improved concoction, unlike any other.

"Thanks, Jason." That's all she could say. She didn't want to say anymore because she might tear up again, not for sadness, but for joy.

After dessert, which everyone raved about, especially with the whipped cream and fudge topping she'd found to drizzle over everything, she put Stina to bed. They all learned a few new swing dance moves. Later, when Jason took Sherrice home, Jill and Bennett talked.

Bennett said he was feeling ambivalent. Jill knew there was no fun in ambivalence. But at least Bennett was trying to express his feelings.

He softly stated, "Jill, I'm not sure where our relationship is going, but I need to back off a little."

Jill wanted to ask, what difference does it make where we're headed, can't we just enjoy the journey? She didn't say that, but she did say, "All that you said may be true, but it still makes me sad. No, actually, it makes me mad!"

They talked a while more, getting nowhere. She was frustrated and she could tell Bennett was uncomfortable as well. After they sat for a while staring at each other, Jill had a good idea. She explained, and they tried out the CRS Stare Off.

That is where Jason found them when he got back home from dropping Sherrice off. He didn't ask, just shook his head and went to bed.

As she continued to sit, Jill found she did become very itchy. Every time Bennett shifted position because of discomfort, she had to smile and think, ah-ha, a point for me. She'd forgotten to go to the bathroom first, and this became a problem for her. Bennett must have noticed, because she saw that his eyes twinkled. She knew he was now thinking he had the upper hand. She wished she'd put a cushion on the chair; her right leg was getting numb. Wait, Bennett looked like he was going to fall asleep. If he did and fell out of the chair, she guessed that would mean she'd won. Her smile got bigger. Bennett's head jerked, and he opened his eyes, remembered what was going on, and sat very straight again. This made Jill laugh. She didn't know whether making noises counted or not, but she had to laugh. Though she really wished she'd gone to the bathroom first, because that urge and laughter were not a good combination. Then Bennett looked at her in such a sweet way that her heart melted. They both smiled.

Bennett said, "On the count of three, up. One…Two…Three."

He stood up. Jill stayed put. That was an old trick, but still a good one.

The laughter was good as it broke the ice. They began to share with each other how hurt they were. Bennett was able to be a little more honest about his need to pull back.

"It's not your thing, it's mine," Bennett admitted. "I'm still conflicted."

Jill pulled Bennett over to the couch and they sat next to each other.

"I'm new to this relationship thing," Jill said, adding, "I've been alone for a long time. It doesn't have to have perfect, I'm learning." She didn't know what else to say.

"It's hard standing here on the middle ground."

"What did you really want to talk about tonight?" Jill asked.

Bennett, looking confused, only said, "I don't know."

Jill softened. He really did look confused. Jill realized things might not go in any special way, and really she didn't have to worry about it, she just needed to let go again and not direct anything.

Jill left the couch and slid a slow CD into the player. She used the bathroom. She felt better. When she came back into the room, Bennett smiled and turned some lights off. They began a slow dance. He held her close with his right hand in the small of her back. He smelled faintly of expensive cologne. Her forehead grazed his smooth cheek. She could feel him inhaling the scent of her hair. She knew why dancing from any distance but arm's length was once considered indecent. It was an excellent aphrodisiac. But right now she mainly felt comforted. She thought this kind of dancing might be better than her idea about the rocking chair therapy. Better, she thought, than anything but laughter. Then she stopped thinking. Lost in a delicious, swaying suspension of time.

WEDNESDAY

The next morning, Jill arrived at work without a care in the world. She'd had a wonderful evening, after all. Donna appeared a little somber when Jill went over to her desk to ask about the day's schedule.

"You okay?" Jill asked.

"I'm not sure how things will end up. The local news called and the guy was talking to Bill earlier. I'm a little worried about yesterday. I can't deny that. I wish I could have intercepted that call about the thing with Ron."

Right then, Bill Bracken stuck his head inside the worker's room. "Donna, may I speak to you for a moment, in my office?"

Jill felt sorry for Donna, who was most always able to be "up" with Bill. His personality was unique and Donna was his antidote. She kept things sane. Right now, as Donna trudged back toward his office, Jill wanted to hug her and say "chin up" or something. But Donna's head was down and Jill couldn't catch her eye.

All Jill's colleagues filtered in. Many times Wednesdays were hard. It wasn't called hump day on a whim. Jill only hoped she'd have no emergencies because, on paper, her points were filled.

Kim, Jill, and Ron talked about the Wedges. Kim said Dean would be able to make a separate visit to the Wedge home. He would help with the initial shock of the death under unusual circumstances. Kim had agreed to officiate at the funeral. Kim had already heard on a phone message from Bill when she'd arrived that even though the funeral was on a Saturday, she and Ron were able to take compensation time to attend. The news media would be there.

"You know, Jill," Kim said, "That's not the funeral I'm worried about. It's the 'roast' that's got me worried."

"That comedian guy that died, Kim?" Jill asked.

"It's coming up tomorrow, and I'm supposed to have some good clean jokes. I have very few, even after asking all the pastors, priests, and chaplains I know. I find the stuff they're giving me is beyond corny or worse. Some of it's very questionable, considering the source. Ron, how about you?"

"I have some knock-knock jokes. But with a guy in a coffin that might not do."

"I'm open to look at anything at this point," Kim conceded. She went to the supply room to return some funeral accouterments.

Ron turned to Jill and said very quietly, "Knock-knock."

"Who's there?" Jill dutifully answered.

"Not so loud. The insurance men might be here."

Jill had no answer. It was so bad that she couldn't even manage a moan.

Jill was surprised when Donna reappeared after a short session with Bill and she looked fine. In fact, she was even smiling. Donna motioned for Jill and Ron to join her over by her desk.

Ron spoke right up. "Bill left me and Kim a message earlier saying that I have to be at the ballpark for the funeral on Saturday, so I know it's not as bad as it could have been."

"I thought there would be some trouble from Bill, but he said he'd gotten a call earlier about the great hospice nurse that helped a patient at the game. I did get in a little hot water for not informing him immediately that you were going to the game. Bill said he pretended to know all about it and the reporter was none the wiser. The really good thing that happened, though, was that after talking to this news guy, Bill found out about some meetings going on over at the veteran's hospital. Now they want Bill to be on some panel show on the local news tonight. Bill's ecstatic."

"Incredible," Jill said, as they all headed to the morning team meeting. Dean was coming out of his little office with the morning snack. Oh, bran muffins and orange slices. What a nice surprise.

Jill walked with him and talked a little about Robert Goulden, about his relationship with his now-deceased renegade father. Though not officially a hospice death, it would affect the patient who was now terminal himself. She repeated some of the history, so Dean would understand.

"Gouldon said he didn't really remember his dad much. His mother was a formal and distant woman who would not speak of the man, except to repeat the fact of the abandonment. After his mother's death, he began to seriously search for answers. Finding nothing, he had imagined a wonderful and fictitious childhood. He said he held a farrago of lovely scenes from literature and film, and heritage became very important to him."

"He probably became very rigid with schedules and an orderly life."

"Yes, that's what he said. Then as an adult, he lost his wife, who died in childbirth. That's when he became a workaholic and made a fortune as a producer in the film industry. In the process of grief, he felt he's not been there for his own son, Bobby."

"Sounds familiar," Dean remarked.

"It does. He finally found his Dad, who ended up being a rascal."

Jill saw how in a few words Dean summed it up. "I'll call him, Jill. You know many of us find a fantasy life to fill in what we are missing."

The team meeting started out on a positive note. Bill's mood was definitely upbeat. In his glory, he began. "Community Hospice will be releasing a press release that Donna and I will prepare regarding the death of our magnificent patient, Mr. Wedge. Aside from that, there's something very exciting on our agenda for today. As you know, in the past the Veterans Administration has been trying to steal our patients."

This was news to all those in the room, not the importance of the agenda, but the part about the vet's hospital trying to steal patients.

Kim, the chaplain, who was on very good terms with Ed Chastell, the VA chaplain, said, "Isn't there enough room for both of our programs?"

"Kim," Bill assured her, "Since I manage this hospice, I should well know that this tactic of theirs is costing us."

"The vets do get a choice," Michelle offered.

"They need to choose us," Bill said, dismissing the comments. "Donna and I will be meeting with a veterans official later this morning. Believe me, we'll get those patients back even if we have to sweeten the deal and offer additional services."

Jill discerned that Bill was offering the team more information than usual. Ordinarily Bill wasn't as expansive with his plans. His normal way was keeping his intentions closer to his chest and then announcing what he'd already done. Jill thought he must be a little worried. Surely he knew the team workers had plenty to do and they weren't interested in hustling up new patients.

Dean addressed Bill's last comment. "All our valued customers must be treated equally. We cannot differentiate amongst the dying."

Bill cast an annoyed look at Dean. It appeared that it was now obvious to him that this wasn't going the way he expected. He officially tapped his papers as a sign he was about to go on to the next subject. However, the other workers, now in a spirit of camaraderie, began to speak up.

Kim said, "Dean made a good point. What goes for one goes for the other."

"I'm a veteran," Ron stated.

"I would like to see us offer additional services to all our patients," Jill remarked.

Ignoring all comments, Bill said, "I think I've made my point."

Lane piped in. "I think Bill has a good point." The rest of the staff looked in unison toward Lane. She hesitated, then said, "OK, I mean everybody here has good points."

"You know, I don't think we need additional services, just the increased use of auxiliary services. Perhaps more volunteers," Donna pondered.

"More bereavement services," Dean offered.

"Enough," Bill stated. "This will be handled by management, and we certainly didn't need everyone on this team to feel the urge to spout off."

Michal Poe

Dr. Almerst looked up from his paperwork after that comment. "That was a bit severe, Bill," he said. "Technically, it is a team."

Bill never seemed to appreciate Almerst's comments, and certainly not when he appeared to weigh in on the side of the workers. Facing the doctor, he rather loudly proclaimed, "Stan, I'm the one who will be doing the bridge building with the Veterans Administration. I'll keep you posted. Moving on, we will now let Lurline give her demonstration on an innovative product to help us in our jobs. Lurline?" He turned toward her not hearing an immediate response."

Lurline looked uncomfortable, as if she sensed danger. She spoke in a hesitant manner as she began to inform Bill that he was mistaken. "Ummm, Bill, wasn't that demonstration on for tomorrow morning? Uhh, unless I'm in error," she added, perkily. "Perhaps it's been changed."

"Yes, yes, of course," Bill covered, adding, "Donna, before we begin our patient review, I'm wondering who is coordinating our community nursing student participation. I haven't seen a new face here at team for over a month."

"They prefer not to come during their school breaks. We're expecting someone today, however. The student should be here before the nurses go into the field."

"Wonderful. Now, nurses," he said, looking toward Ron and Jill with his pasted-on smile, "Don't fight over who gets to take someone out and show them how a top-rate hospice is run."

Jill and Ron didn't comment. Jill knew Lane was exempt from preceptoring, since she hadn't finished her first year as a full-time employee. Jill sighed. Ron had taken the last student nurse out. She wondered if this would mean she'd get an extra point under the new system. Although she loved her job and liked to mentor, she knew that having a student along would slow her down.

She keenly remembered her day under the aegis of a home health nurse in her student days. At first the nurse seemed rather mean toward Jill. But in retrospect, Jill had understood she'd only been protective of her patients and was overwhelmed as it was. The thing that had impressed Jill was how hard that nurse had worked for her patients. The very first patient they'd seen that day, many years ago, was a middle-aged woman, still living alone. It was a very hot day, and there was no air conditioner in the home. The nurse wanted to get the patient as comfortable as possible. So she'd asked the patient if she had a fan. Then she crawled around in an old storeroom near a back bedroom, found what she needed and set the fan up. After that she got the patient a large pitcher of water. She'd found a rolling pin and an old towel and pounded the ice into chips. This nurse had been sent out to insert a urinary catheter, to save the woman's strength from getting up and down from the bedside commode and stop the leakage accidents she was having. Because the woman was very heavy, the nurse couldn't maneuver from the side of the bed, so she got up on the bed, as if it was the most normal thing in the world, and got the right leverage. That way she was able to introduce the catheter in an easier way. Before they left the house, the nurse was dripping drops of sweat from the heat and her exertion, but the patient was so much more comfortable. Throughout the entire visit, the nurse had kept up a pleasant chatter, and the patient's dignity had remained intact.

Michal Poe

Jill could only hope she always gave as good or even a better experience for the many students she'd dragged around with her from time to time.

Jill's attention was drawn back into the present when she heard that only patients with serious concerns were to be reviewed this morning. These included Jill's patient, Mr. Bob Dobson. There was worry that the staff never knew for sure where he was located. Jill and Michelle agreed to set up an appointment for Thursday with various family members. Then Stan reported that Mr. Robert Goulden had come in for a co-consultation with him and Dr. Rens. That patient's cancer was in the liver, certainly a cirrhosis connection. His complexion was already looking sallow, and that meant he probably didn't have as much time left to live as he'd expected. Dr. Almerst said the news was taken well, and Robert's grown son, who was with him, had immediately insisted on hiring a private nurse. Though Robert didn't see the need, he'd capitulated. Dr. Almerst thought that with follow-up calls, weekly visits were adequate for now.

Bill was champing at the bit to prepare himself for his ten o'clock meeting with the public relations representative from Veterans Affairs. In fact, as the meeting was breaking up, Bill's last words to Donna were, "Look out for that guy Chambers from the vets."

Several, but not Bill, heard Donna's questionable comment, "Did I hear a please?"

***

Back in their workspace, everyone relaxed and started loading up in order to leave. Ron thought he heard something. "Shush a minute," he said. "Hear that?" They all heard it now. It was the sound of tinkling bells, followed by a light knock. Sandy went to the outer door and escorted a very young, rather embarrassed, student nurse into the workroom. She wore metal jangling earrings, bracelets that made more noise, and enough metal around her neck to sink a body in salt water.

Donna went to the student's side, saying, "You must be Aliasha. Welcome. Jill, here's your student for today."

Jill smiled, thinking, well she won't be hard to keep track of, all belled up like a Judas goat. She knew the younger nursing students were nothing like the group she went to school with. Less than twenty years, but seemingly centuries divided the classes.

Jill introduced the student to several team members, then sat her down with a policy book and a few of the patients' records. Jill's first visit would be to Melissa Sanchez. She was a young patient, comparatively new to hospice. This would be a good introduction, and Jill thought Melissa would like the distraction of having a younger nurse along as well. She also planned on seeing Randy Jones at Hope House. That was a unique living arrangement and would showcase the variety of types of patients and living conditions the hospice nurses encountered. Along with a few ordinary revisits, that should make a good day for both of them.

Before Jill and Aliasha left, however, Donna took Jill aside. "I have a favor to ask you, Jill," Donna said. "After your first visit, I've asked Ron to take the student on one visit, as Bill wants a nurse to sit in on the vets meeting. He's being so aggressive. I think it would be good if you did join in. It'll help me a lot," Donna added.

It was an additional complication, but Jill agreed to get back as soon as her first visit was finished. She was worried about Donna, who seemed a bit over-burdened today. This would be a way she could be helpful and repay all the wonderful things Donna did on behalf of the nurses.

On the way to the first visit, Jill didn't have much time to talk to her student because of all the speakerphone messages and even a personal call from Jason. She told him she'd call later and wondered how he was able to call before mid-morning. It was a good education for the nursing students to know how busy the job could get. To her credit, Aliasha didn't text message once during the drive. In fact, she appeared to be paying close attention and even finished reading Melissa's chart.

***

Melissa's teenage son was practicing his skateboard moves in front of the Sanchez home. As Jill and Aliasha started through the front gate, they saw a man driving off in a big hurry.

"Raul," Jill addressed the teen in a very loud voice, seeing he was wearing earbuds, "Was that your dad leaving?"

"Yeah," Raul answered, removing his electronic gear from his head and sticking them in his top pocket.

Jill knew she'd have to ask some specific question to get more information. "What are you doing home, and is your dad doing okay today?"

Raul answered as he went back to continuing to perfect his jumps. "I'm off school today. Dad's been feeling the need to get out. Said he just couldn't take it any more. So I'm in charge. He said I can get him back here if you need him now."

"No," Jill answered. "We'll go see what we can do. Thanks."

Raul jumped off his board and opened the door, skateboard in hand. Everyone heard Melissa crying. Aliasha gasped, but then she curtailed her emotions. This was a good sign; she was following Jill's lead.

Jill remained calm. "I'll take good care of her, Raul. But before I forget, here's the booklet your dad wanted me to bring by for you."

"Ummm," Raul said as he stuffed it in his back pocket, not even reading the title, *How Teens View Illness*. He took his earbuds from his shirt pocket and reinserted them. He resumed his skateboard practice down the long driveway as Jill and Aliasha entered through the front door.

Jill allowed her helper to carry her equipment bag into the back bedroom.

Melissa, with long, thin hair, sat up in bed. She reached out toward Jill. Between sobs, she blurted out, "Oh, nurse, it's my hair. Jill, nobody told me it would happen so fast. The doctor said this kind of chemo might not even hurt my hair. My eyebrows are already gone. It's creeping everybody out."

"Wow," Jill said softly.

Melissa yelled, "My sister Maria said, 'It'll grow back and maybe it'll be curly.' I don't want curly. I want my hair!" She resumed crying and was really loud.

Jill pulled up a chair for the student and then sat on the side of Melissa's bed. She sat close so that Melissa could resume clutching her hand. Jill had been through this many times, with many patients—this anger, this feeling of humiliation. What was there to do but work through it? When Melissa calmed a little, Jill felt the need to reach out and touch Melissa's hair.

Melissa, noticing, said, "See, I'm so weak I couldn't even get out to get it cut before it thinned. I should just get the scissors and chop it all off."

She sobbed a little more, and when things quieted down again, Jill asked softly, "Do you know how I earned part of my way through nursing school?"

Melissa looked up, "Barbering?" she asked, hopefully.

Jill smiled.

They all went into the bathroom. After washing up and putting towels around Melissa's neck, Jill gave Melissa a cute, short haircut. Jill made it fun by using Aliasha as her assistant, calling out for the scissors, comb, water glass, etc. Soon they were all laughing, and Melissa said she was going to find an old picture for Jill, next time she came, in which she had her hair the same style after Raul was born.

After taking another look in the hand mirror, she said disparagingly, "But the eyebrows…"

Aliasha spoke up. "This reminds me of that old, old sitcom, you know, where Elaine drew on Uncle Leo's eyebrows!"

"*Seinfeld*?" Melissa offered.

"'Old, old sitcom'?" Jill protested.

"That was one of my favorite episodes, until now," Melissa lamented.

"Okay, let's do it!" Jill proclaimed.

Aliasha took Melissa's eyebrow pencil, and after taking off several pieces of her jewelry that were obviously going to get in the way, she begin drawing various eyebrows on Melissa. Some looked sad, some silly or happy, and some mad. With each set, and before it was washed off for the next, all the women continuously broke out in hysterical laughter. Aliasha finally got just the right angle and things were looking good.

They heard a knock on the door and Raul's tentative voice, "Dad's back early, and he wanted me to ask, is everything all right in there?"

"Tell Daddy everything is fine, Honey. Just fine," Melissa answered.

***

After the home visit and in the car on the way back to the office, Jill and Aliasha had time to talk. Aliasha was impressed with the honest communication that ensued after the beauty regimen. Husband and son had sat in the bedroom toward the end of the visit and talked for a while. The patient had been left in a good place, emotionally and physically.

"I didn't know things could get so personal," Aliasha commented.

"It's a fine line," Jill acknowledged. "You did a good job for the first patient, Aliasha."

"I tried to follow your mood. I wasn't sure which way things would go."

"That's really important. Sometimes when things are really crazy, only the nurse's calm presence can settle things down. There are many times you don't know where things will go; it's like riding a bucking horse—you just hang on for a while."

"Until the clowns come out to save you?" Aliasha asked.

Jill laughed. She liked Aliasha. She was top-rate nursing material. With every bell removed, and Aliasha was just now taking out one pair of her large hoop earrings, Jill felt her becoming wiser. But that was all illusion, and didn't this job teach you to not look to the outer but probe the inner?

After a few minutes of silence, Aliasha spoke. "I remember when my brother was in the hospital." As she spoke, she put her hand up toward her face. "He was in turmoil, and one nurse came in and put a chair right up close to him and asked him how she could help…and really listened to him. I don't think anything was changed in medicines or anything, except he felt cared for." Out of the corner of her eye, Jill could see Aliasha wipe away a tear.

"Uh-huh…" Jill murmured, feeling there was an important story behind that revelation.

"My brother died in that hospital, all alone," Aliasha went on. "That's what made me decide to be a nurse."

"How long ago?" Jill asked after an appropriate pause. She was hoping it wasn't really recent, as doing hospice work too soon could complicate things for Aliasha.

"Five years," she answered, "but it never stops hurting."

They were quiet as Jill drove on toward the office. After a while, Aliasha lightened the mood by asking, "Did you really work as a barber when you were going to nursing school? I can barely make it through now, studying all day."

"Just for a short time one summer. I was an assistant. It was a necessity to earn a little money. I learned to cut and style, but it wasn't actually in a barber shop."

"Huh?"

"It was at Doggie Do's Mobile Grooming!"

***

Ron looked up when he saw Jill and Aliasha laughing as they were getting out of the Jeep. Jill knew Ron had borrowed Donna's car, because he could hardly ask Aliasha to ride on the back of his motorcycle for their co-visit. Although after getting to know her, Jill was sure Aliasha would've been up for it.

Jill went directly to the meeting, noticing she was about ten minutes late. She looked forward to sinking down into one of the comfortable, plush leather chairs. An extra desk chair had been pulled into Bill's very nice office. Donna sat in it, with a pad and pen in her lap. Donna's chair sat farther back. She was not looking terribly pleased. In fact, when Jill entered after a quiet knock and Donna saw Jill, her face lit up. Jill didn't want to be called upon for too much duty. It was hard to read Bill. Donna did it best. Jill was mostly there to support Donna, she reminded herself.

Bill Bracken was sitting at his desk across from the veteran's official, Mr. Chambers, who was dressed in a suit and had a wire in his ear. This official, Jill couldn't help notice, was even better dressed than Bill. It looked like these two were obviously cut from the same tailor's cloth.

"Jill. One of our wonderful nurses!" Bill exclaimed, as Jill took her chair. It seemed he would use this interruption as a way to reiterate the point he'd been trying to make. "This is Mr. Chambers from the VA. I've been telling him that the local hospices would benefit from a committee to look into disbursement of the burgeoning baby boomer veterans who will be using these services over the next few decades."

Mr. Chambers waved his hand, dismissing that sentiment. "Mr. Bracken, we already have our plan worked out and are expecting to accommodate that need."

"Surely you'd like to have the hospice consortium group involved in that planning?" Bill pressed.

"Not really," Mr. Chambers answered.

"But think of the goodwill generated by—"

Jill could tell Bill wanted to really hammer in his point. However, he was interrupted mid-sentence by a phone call the official was taking through his earpiece. Jill was surprised the man didn't even excuse himself. He just began to talk even as Bill was speaking. "Right-o. We'll take a meeting with the councilman in about…" he checked his watch, "…ten minutes."

Mr. Chambers ended the call and stood up, demonstrating that he was ready to end the meeting.

Bill's face reddened; he was obviously upset by the official's rudeness. "We'll just cut to the chase," Bill said, louder than was necessary, "Stop stealing our patients. This government interference has got to stop. Don't we pay enough taxes as it is?"

Chambers looked shocked and then frowned. He didn't answer but left in a real hurry after throwing a few of his business cards on a side table as he walked out the door.

Donna called after him, "I'll mail you that consortium list." Then she turned toward her boss saying, "Bill! That was hardly bridge building."

Bill, who now appeared a little embarrassed, looked down at his expensive shoes. Then he commented upon the official's footwear. "Harrumph, maybe he didn't think I'd know Bruno Magli loafers when I saw them."

Jill left the office while Donna and Bill rehearsed for the five o'clock news show.

She packed up some supplies and got out of the office without further complications. She finished an easy revisit and then stopped for lunch. She treated herself to pizza; she really hadn't gotten any the night before.

Before she could pick up Aliasha for the Hope House visit, she got a call from Michelle. "Janice Stearn is in the hospital. She's giving everyone fits. I'm on my way; can you come?"

I'll delay one visit and see if I can postpone another. Did they say what she's in for?"

"Her doctor got a call from airport security. Janice had fainted or something."

"Here we go again," Jill said. "That woman was probably trying to do jumping jacks."

"She won't be doing those now."

"What do you mean?" Jill asked.

"They have her in restraints."

"I'll be right there," Jill assured Michelle.

On the way to the hospital, she finished her phone calls and left a message to let Aliasha know that when she was through with the visit with Ron she was to meet Jill at the Hope House and that wouldn't be until three or three-thirty. She also got ahold of Jason, who reminded Jill that today was the last school holiday of the year.

"Oh," Jill said, "I forgot. What are you doing?"

"Until you called, I was sleeping. But I'm gonna go shoot some baskets."

"And?" Jill asked, waiting to hear the right answer.

"And, pick up that stuff from the garden list you left?"

"Good answer. Bye, son, I love you." Maybe it was overkill, but she was always in the habit of saying 'love you' while saying goodbye to everyone she cared about. It was probably the business she was in that made things seem more immediate.

***

Michal Poe

Janice hadn't yet been admitted to the hospital. She was still in the emergency department when Jill got there. The head nurse told Jill a bed would be available soon, but Mrs. Stearn would need a sitter to watch over her erratic behavior.

When Jill entered the little alcove room, she saw that Michelle was there. She and a hospital nurse were untying Janice.

Michelle addressed the patient, "You know, Janice, if you try and hit anyone else, the restraints will have to go back on."

"She was trying to give me a shot against my will. That's battery!" Janice exclaimed.

"Technically, it's assault," Michelle said. Seeing Jill, she added, "Jill, I promised the doctor I'd stay here until the sitter could be arranged. Is there any way you can go down to the business office? The ER admitting clerk is in a snit. The nurse said Janice has no insurance. Some mistake, I guess."

Janice was still yelling, through her pursed lips, "I have everything paid up in advance. If all these incompetents worked in my office, they'd be fired."

Ignoring the yelling, Jill answered, "Sure, Michelle. I'll be back soon."

As she made her way out of the room, she heard the conversation begin between Michelle and Janice. Michelle had turned her full attention to Janice and asked, "Can we talk?"

"Do I have a choice?" Janice asked sarcastically, but at least she spoke in a fairly normal voice.

"You keep overdoing it, and now you've ended up in the hospital."

"That idiot at the airport dragged me here. This time I wasn't overdoing it."

"You weren't?"

"I always promised myself when I hit the glass ceiling, I'd go back to Baltimore."

Jill now out of earshot, went farther down the hall and entered the business office. Two people were leaving; they looked rather grim and were shaking their heads. That didn't bode well. However, Jill was a champ at bureaucracy. She took a number and got fourteen. The screen said they were on number six, and the clock said one-forty-nine. Ten minutes later, number seven was called. Jill decided to get over to the bathroom, since this was going to take a while. When she returned, after stopping by the coffee kiosk machine to get a latte to go, it was only ten minutes after two, and the screen said number fifteen!

Jill went to the counter, and handed over her number, saying, "I'm sorry to bother you, but I had to leave for a few minutes and you were only on number seven."

"We don't have numbers eight through thirteen," the clerk said in the most matter-of-fact manner. "I'll make an exception and take you out of order after the next patron. As a courtesy to others, please take care of your other business before you come in here."

Jill didn't argue. She had to wait another ten minutes. At least she was glad she got to finish her coffee. When called, she took the chair across from the partition.

"I need to establish that a patient has medical insurance," she said.

"Social security number?"

Jill took out her data page from Janice Stearn's chart and pushed it over so the clerk could see it, asking, "Is there any more preliminary info you need?"

"What are you here for?" The clerk asked

"I need to establish a patient's medical insurance coverage." Jill repeated.

"Not yours?"

"She's in the emergency room now. Cubicle 4-A."

The clerk looked up and noticed Jill's ID badge. She shook her head. "As a health professional, surely you must know that privacy laws won't allow me to give you any information."

"But," Jill began to protest.

"Take this form up to her and at least get her initials, in front of someone signing as a witness, then come back and take a number."

"Another number?"

"Just so no one will think you're getting out of line. Get my attention and I will take you next."

"Thanks," Jill said in a heartfelt manner.

When Jill returned to the ER, Janice was on her cell phone and Michelle was filling out her paperwork. The head nurse looked in as well, saying, "Good, I see it's all quiet in here."

Jill got Janice's attention by waving the form and tried to hand it off to Janice. "Initials," Jill said.

Janice shook her head; she was arguing with someone on the telephone. It was an intense conversation, and Jill thought it was a customer. Janice made a scribbling sign with her hand and motioned towards Michelle. Michelle signed and nodded toward Jill. Jill returned the nod and put Janice's initials on the form.

Michelle shrugged. "We'll probably end up in hell for some of the illegal stuff we do for our patients," she said quietly.

Janice heard and yelled "Maybe we're in hell already!" Then, returning to her phone call, she said, "No, I did not say that to you." Janice fumbled around with the phone for a minute and then threw it in her purse. "Damn battery."

Jill was only too happy to head back to the clerk. She really didn't have all afternoon for this. Again she met a sad-looking patient coming out of the office, this one had a sweater over her pinned-up hospital gown, and she too was shaking her head. Inside, the screen said number twenty-one. That was good, since she'd pulled number twenty before she'd left to go back to Janice's room. But the clerk that served her was gone. She pulled another number, just in case. It was ten! Somehow the missing numbers had reappeared. The new clerk called "Number twenty-one." There was no one else in the waiting room. Jill approached the partition. She gave the clerk her numbers. The clerk looked at them very closely.

"Out of courtesy to others, you need to be here when your number is called."

Jill smiled weakly. She was wise enough to know it was better she not say anything. She gave the completed form to the clerk.

"Has this case already been opened?"

"I was in here earlier, and…"

"What was the clerk's name?"

"I don't know."

This clerk looked hard at Jill's badge. She said, "Always get the name of those you work with. I'm surprised to have to tell you that."

Jill took a breath. She noted the clerk's badge and said, "Yes, thank you, Marella."

"I have to leave now; the girl who served you will be back from break soon. It's best to wait for her." The clerk had risen and was on her way out the back.

Jill was now alarmed, "Do I have to take another number?" she called out, desperate to get something done.

Marella stopped in her tracks then turned and looked directly at Jill. "Dear, you're the only person in here, why would you think you'd need to get yet another number?" Then she was gone.

Jill sat rather stunned for a few seconds. Suddenly she saw a horde of people coming in the door. She raced to the number dispenser and grabbed a number, barely beating a man on crutches. It was number twenty-two. Ten very long minutes passed and the other clerk returned. Jill brought her form up and handed it to "Clara." Jill made a mental note of the name.

Clara looked it over briefly, then she typed in the patient's full name. She paused a moment and then turned the computer monitor around so Jill could see it. "See. Right here it shows Ms. Stearn has full coverage. In fact, she's paid ahead. We don't have time for unnecessary nonsense. Why were you sent here anyway?"

"I don't know, I really don't know," Jill, the previous bureaucracy champion, said. She walked out with a grim look on her face, shaking her head.

Jill returned to the ER feeling discouraged. Michelle must have noticed because she quietly said, "You look a little spacey, are you overtired?"

Jill shook her head. "Michelle, I don't know how you do it day after day, dealing with all these agencies, all this paperwork you do. It was so exasperating, a fiasco, in that admitting office."

"It's my early-morning rides on my horses. Clears my head."

"Even after the late nights with the cowboys?"

Michelle laughed, then said, "Jill, the doctor is not sure now whether to admit Janice or not."

Jill nodded and told Michelle, "We need to stay longer anyway; I need to catch my breath."

Janice was trying to get dressed, and she didn't look happy.

Jill knew better than argue about her actions. "Janice," Jill asked, "I meant to ask about Baltimore. What's in Baltimore?"

"It's *who's* in Baltimore. He's the love of my life."

"You wanted to see him?"

"The man has waited for me for twenty years."

"Ahh," Jill commented.

"One more time. I just want to see him one more time. I didn't know I was going to hit the mortality ceiling this year."

After a few seconds passed in silence, Michelle said, "Janice, do you think he would come to you?"

"Yes," Janice said. "But it doesn't seem right to have it happen that way."

Jill handed her cell phone over to Janice. "Let him decide."

Jill and Michelle had a quiet conversation together. There was no privacy in the little curtained off area, but while Janice was on the phone, they tried to create a semblance of one.

Janice handed the cell phone back to Jill. "He's flying in tomorrow. Jill, help me get back to my home. The doctors always think I'm crazy."

Jill smiled and gave Janice a little hug. "Okay, I'll get a hold of the doctor for discharge. No more long work hours, right? The nurse's report shows better oxygen intake now. Is your pain level still okay?"

"Yes, no pain. I've retired as of today. Jill…" Janice blinked away a few tears. "Thanks."

Jill put her arm around Janice. "You're a brave one, Janice. May I meet him sometime?"

Janice gave an almost shy smile, saying, "You might even be matron of honor at the wedding."

On the way out, after getting things arranged so that Janice could get back home, Jill knew that Michelle wondered how she'd fared in the business office. Jill relayed the story. Michelle laughed knowingly.

"I think the insurance thing will show up on the computer now. Also, I just had to find out what was in Baltimore," Jill said.

"I knew you were going to get to the bottom of it."

Jill's mood was now improved. She and Michelle talked about other bureaucracy snafus they'd encountered. In fact she laughed all the way to the parking lot. Michelle continued to chuckle in sympathy.

At her car, Michelle pulled out some information to give to Jill. "You're going by the Hope House, right?"

"Yes," Jill replied, "I'm seeing Randy. The student will be there too."

"Remember Jerome? He's my patient from a couple of years ago. We graduated him and he's doing pretty good still. He wanted this revised 'Intimacy and Illness,' brochure. Would you hand it off?"

"Sure. I might read it first though."

"Bennett?" Michelle asked cryptically.

"No, I'm beginning to think it's me," Jill replied, more serious than she'd let Michelle see her in quite a while.

"Are you doing anything tonight?" Michelle asked.

"No. No fireworks and that's the problem. Bennett's getting tired of waiting."

"I mean, are you *going* anywhere tonight?"

Jill shook her head, as she knew her face must have reddened. "Nothing that I know of."

"Meet me at Dano's," Michelle said while starting up her car. "I'm giving my line-dancing class, and Lurline is coming too. It'll be a lot of fun. We can talk after."

"Maybe, but I might have to make babysitting arrangements for Mom."

"Good then, it's settled." Michelle put her pickup in reverse, and speaking louder over the engine she called out, "Lesson at seven-thirty, then the fun resumes at eight. It's best if you wear cowboy boots. I'll bring that pair for you."

"Those were too big…and…," Jill tried to protest.

Michelle interrupted, "No buts!" She threw her last comment over her shoulder as she took off: "Don't worry, your feet will be swollen by that time."

Shaking her head again, Jill took the brochure and headed toward her last visit. Truth was, she realized, she needed a night out; her run would have to wait another day.

***

Michal Poe

Aliasha met Jill in the vestibule of the old mansion, right on time. Hope House was a building in the downtown area that had been renovated for younger, chronically ill persons who had no other resources. They shared kitchen and clean-up duties and helped care for one another as they were able. The paid staff was bare bones. Jill was pleased that her hospice had, more than fifteen years ago, responded to this need and helped with the renovation. Ramps, elevators, large doorways, and other changes were accomplished with taste. This still left the large house looking beautiful. Most of the patients who were moved into hospice care there were so-called charity cases. Even those with state and county insurance found their plans wouldn't begin to pay for full medication and care needs. Therefore, a large part of the expense was paid out of several different organizations' indigent fees. Everyone was treated with respect, and Jill found it truly a hopeful house. The building looked about the same over the years, but the types of patients inhabiting it had changed. At one time the majority were AIDS patients, now they were the minority, due to the increase in medicines that helped stay the ravages of that disease.

Aliasha had put some of her jewelry back on, and the jingling was pleasant in that atmosphere. Jill hadn't been there but a scintilla, and in fact she was signing the guest book in the entry when she was yahooed by Jerome. He was in a wheelchair and barreled toward her.

"Jill! Jill, remember me? I graduated from hospice over two years ago and look at me now." He did a wheelie that almost made Jill's heart stop. He was leaning very far back and then maneuvered his wheel chair around her in the entry. He added, "See? You're not always right."

Jill had to laugh at his exuberance. "How could I forget you, Jerome?" she practically squealed. They embraced like long-lost friends.

"You brought Tinkerbell along," he continued. "She's beautiful!" He laughed and put his hand out for Aliasha. She was game, bless her heart, Jill thought. Aliasha shook his hand and then waggled her bells a little louder.

Even at his sickest, Jerome had such *joie de vivre.* He was one of those people with whom she wished she could have kept up a friendship. However, that was a definite no-no and would have crossed the professional line. Forming true friendships with patients, even former patients, changed the relationship. It would be thought that the patient was taking advantage of the nurse, but it was just the opposite. The nurses and other workers knew that the patients they met were from all walks of life. It made the job so rich, so interesting. The patients, however, were a captive audience, and very dependent on the professionalism and the objectivity of their hospice team. She made a mental note to make sure to discuss that a little with Aliasha before the day was over.

Jerome continued to chatter away as he wheeled his chair alongside them in the wide hallway. Soon Jill was up to date on his life. When they reached the end of the hallway, where she needed to find her patient's room, she took a break in the conversation to pull out the information that Michelle had given her for him. As she handed it over, he grabbed it, and knowing Jill was there to see someone else, he turned a few more circles around Jill and Aliasha and sped away toward the recreation room, saying, "Tell Michelle thanks."

As Jill referred to Randy Jones's folder there in the hallway, Aliasha asked, "Two years—how do you even remember him?"

"Some just stick with you."

Jill and Aliasha stopped by the first door and used the hallway restroom to wash up. Coming out they noticed an ornate chess set dominated a friendly corner in the recreation room. That was where Jerome had parked himself, already busily reading the brochure. They proceeded down the right corridor and found the doorway number they needed. Even though the room's door was open, Jill gave a knock before they went inside. Randy's partner, Roger, was getting him out of bed and into a wheelchair. Jill helped with the transfer as she introduced Aliasha.

How's it going, Randy?" Jill asked as she removed her equipment from her bag.

Randy gave a little smile. Roger answered for him. "We're pretty good, Jill. There's a problem with staff turnover lately. So everyone is looking out for everybody else. We all try to do little things for each other."

"That's good." Then Jill turned to Randy, asking, "It's such a nice day, want to get out in the sunshine a little?"

When he nodded his consent, Aliasha took charge. "May I push you?"

"Sure, do that for him," Roger said as he opened the sliding patio doors. Outside they had a view of a little flower garden. The four of them sat there for a minute, enjoying the sunshine.

Randy took a breath of the fresh air. "This is nice."

After a few more minutes, Jill quietly began her assessment, checking the vital signs and getting some questions answered. Aliasha kept Roger talking. Jill knew she was doing it so Randy could answer the questions honestly. That girl was perceptive.

"Jill do you know what I did?" Randy asked.

"No, what?"

"I mixed up our medications again. At this point I don't think it matters."

"It matters to me, Randy. I'll leave another medicine box." She pulled one out of her bag. "I'll write Roger's name on this one, so you'll know which is which. I'll help you fill them before I leave. What else is going on?"

Randy didn't answer that question. He had a far off look in his eyes, so Jill was quiet.

She heard the quiet conversation between Aliasha and Roger.

Roger was speaking quietly, but Jill knew Randy could hear him too.

"I was always the sick one. I kept a cold, had bad eyes. He was the super-stud. What a shock when my anchor, my rock started to crumble. Seems like we've always been together. He told me last night he thought I would be all right…you know, without him. I question his faith on that. I don't know how he expects me to go on."

Aliasha didn't say anything, but put her hand on his arm. Roger pulled out a tissue from his back pocket and blew his nose.

Finally Randy spoke again to Jill. "You know, at first we hoped for a cure. Then we decided it would be good to stay real comfortable. Now we're about to settle for not becoming helpless, drooling idiots." Jill saw the corners of his mouth twitch as though he was suppressing a smile.

"Oh, Randy," Jill said.

"I think we might make that last goal. At least one of us will. Thanks for thinking to get me out in the sunshine, Jill, it feels so good," he said, smiling at last.

After the visit, Jill sat in her car and talked with Aliasha for a while. Jill let her know that she thought she had the instincts for this type of job. Aliasha said she felt comfortable with these patients. She said she really liked the few quiet times and following the patient's lead.

"You know, I see that nursing is not all about doing things and making people face reality all the time," she said.

Jill understood her meaning. She agreed that unless the patients were making decisions that were actually harmful to them or their loved ones, they had a right to their feelings and actions.

"They don't always need total direction," Jill said.

Alicia nodded. "That's good, you know, the not always handing out more advice."

Jill was pleased with Aliasha's insightful comments. Jill talked about maintaining boundaries and how that was sometimes difficult. How the rule about not socializing with the patients became a little awkward at times, especially in a smaller community such as Burnhills. Then they reviewed the day, with Jill answering a few of Aliasha's other questions, including letting her know it was okay to organize the medicine boxes for patients.

Aliasha revealed what Roger had told her right before they left. "He said, 'When Randy does die, if you were to tap on my heart, you would only hear a hollow sound.' That's so sad," she added.

"And so lovely," Jill remarked, "to have a love that deep."

Jill checked off Aliasha's checklist for her class assignment. Then they both went their separate ways.

***

Back in the office, everyone was there. They wanted to support Donna and watch the five o'clock news with her to catch Bill's discussion about hospice. Ron and Lane were at the worktable finishing up their charting.

When Jill had arrived, the first thing Ron asked was, "How did Jangles do with you?" He added, "I think she was good on the visit we did together."

"You didn't call her that did you?"

"Yeah, she liked it. She has a little rock band called QuirkySludge and she's going to use Jangles as her tag now."

"Wow," Jill said. "I tell you, she was my bright spot today."

Ron nodded in agreement and then they got busy working on their charting.

"Jill," Ron said, "Since I'm off all next week…"

"Oh, don't remind me." Jill groaned.

"Well, they'll have substitutes for some of the visits. But I've already checked with Donna, and rather than have you open new people next week you're going to take over some of the more difficult ones I have."

"Whoopee."

"Chase Miller, for one. I want you go out with me tomorrow and I'll introduce you. You can probably handle that mother of his. I can't."

"I'll do what I can Ron. I hate you when you leave though."

"The feeling is mutual when you leave."

Donna announced to all that the unit count looked very good for yesterday and Bill was pleased to see how productive everyone had been. "Don't forget today's sheets," she added.

Michelle and Ron smiled at one another. They'd been talking earlier and realized that yesterday they'd both seen one fewer patient than usual. However, with the extra mileage, lab drop-offs, literature disbursements, supply pickups, and other extras usually not counted, their sheets looked great.

Lurline stopped by Jill's desk to ask her what she was going to wear dancing. "That's one place where those peasant skirts of yours would look good," she said.

"One place?" Jill inquired.

"Oh, you know what I mean. I think we're gonna slay those cowboys." Lurline winked, "We'll be a phalanges of death."

"Cowboys? Those guys are probably office workers who think they're hot in jeans," Jill offered.

"That's all right too, as long as they actually do look good in jeans."

Lurline went over and volunteered to help Ron and Lane set up a small television on Donna's desk.

Jill finished her work and made a quick call home. Jason said he'd let the day care know he could pick Stina up at nine or ten so she could enjoy her night out.

"Could you possibly get her a little earlier?" Jill asked.

"No, Mom," Jason answered. "Hey, remember, I have a life now."

"Fully supported by your mother's sacrifice," Jill quipped before hanging up. She was so grateful to be on good terms and have the honest communication she was able to enjoy with her son. It was one less stress.

The workers crowded around the television to watch the five o'clock news. While the national review was on, Jill asked Donna how the rehearsal went with Bill.

"Good," Donna said. "Bill was able to make a few good points. I was pretending to be a hostile debater. I thought he did well. Hope he keeps his head though. If we come off good, it will be great public relations for our annual fund-raiser coming up."

"That man blows hot," Sandy commented. No one argued.

All were quiet as the "Sunset Show" segment began. The host sat in the middle between Mr. Chambers, the VA official, and Bill. During the on-air introductions, the host mangled Bill's last name. He called him Mr. Blackett, from a "local hospice."

Donna looked distressed to see that both men wore red ties, blue shirts, and dark gray suits.

"What a bad coincidence," she said. "Especially since I advised Bill about colors that would look good on TV."

Chambers scooted closer to the host. Bill did the same. The two guests were already looking a little strange, since they were dressed alike. Both had big, wide, fake, friendly-looking smiles. They looked like bobble-headed bookends.

The host began in a dramatic manner and voice. "Our topic today is the business of death. We have two knowledgeable men here to talk to us about hospice. Gentlemen, since death numbers are growing, is hospice care the next big business? Mr. Chambers?"

"I don't know whether we should call it a business," Chambers replied. "But it's our administration's goal to take care of our own and offer the best end-of-life care possible."

"And…" Bill began.

The host had turned his face fully toward Chambers and away from Bill.

"Mr. Chambers, please finish that thought."

"Certainly. I'm happy to use your wonderful show to announce that we are about to begin a campaign to build a hospice wing onto our new facility. We'll be able to accommodate our veterans in comfort and allow…"

"The consortium…" Bill did his best to get a word in edgewise.

"A whole wing for the terminally ill? Viewers, you heard it here," the host said loudly. "The veteran's hospital will have the latest in end-of-life care, right here in our fair city."

Bill tried again, "I'd like to comment on…"

"Let me ask you, sir," the host had his total attention focused on Chambers, "How many vets can this wing handle?"

At this point, it seemed like Bill had had it. "Mr. Chambers," he said, speaking rapidly and somewhat loudly, "Would that vet's wing admit your mother if she were ill?"

"His mother?" The host looked confused.

"My mother?" Chambers echoed.

"Your mama." Bill said, even louder. "You see, that's my point. The veterans are only a small part of the baby boomer generation that is scheduled to die."

"'Scheduled to die'?" The host repeated, incredulous. He turned toward Chambers as if to ask for help.

Chambers abruptly jumped to his feet. "My mama? My mama is in good health, I'll have you know."

"That's what everybody thinks, until they're told they're terminal!" Bill yelled, and stood almost nose to nose with Chambers.

Jill - Hospice Nurse, Book Two: Last Exit

The camera tried to pull in close to the host's face, although the viewers could still hear and see activity on either side of him. Attempting to speak in his normal announcing tone, the host said, "We're all out of time for tonight because of the breaking news story, upcoming…soon. Thanks for watching."

"Cut!" someone yelled, before the screen faded into a commercial.

Shock was registered on the faces of the workers in the hospice room. Donna actually groaned. In silence, Ron unplugged the television and set it back in the cupboard.

Donna recovered slightly and weakly said, "This can be fixed."

It was a nice thing to say. Even though Jill thought Donna had said it to try to convince herself. At least Bill was introduced as a local hospice director, no mention of their name, Community Hospice. Still, Jill was mortified as she realized everyone's destinies were tied together. She knew she'd never be worried about a job. Nursing meant security. But her little place where she thought she was doing the best nursing she'd ever done, could that be at risk? If Bill went down, he'd take their hospice with him.

The hospice workers trudged out of the office. This was the second night in a row they'd had a shock.

***

Before Jill took off for home, she heard a tap on her window. Lurline made the motion to roll down the window.

"Jill, I just want you to know that Lane found out about the girl's night outing and invited herself along."

Now it seemed it was Jill's turn to groan.

Michal Poe

Lane was so much younger that the rest of them. Jill knew Lane wanted to fit in, but she just didn't. Her values, her interests, were all so different. Jill felt it wasn't that Lane wanted the company of the rest of them, she just didn't want to be left out.

"Oh, Lurline, that's all I need," Jill lamented.

"Well I could hardly refuse her. The fact that she's Donna's niece makes it doubly hard to exclude her, you know."

It was true, that fact didn't sit well with others in the office. No matter how much they respected Donna, Lane wasn't fully trusted yet. Plus she'd been hired right out of nursing school with no real experience, and at times it showed. Often the other nurses, and sometimes the office staff, had to pick up the slack.

"Oh, crap. What a day," Jill sighed. "Okay, I'll see you later, Lurline. Thanks for letting me know."

As Jill drove home, she really wished she hadn't agreed to the evening so readily. Hell, Lane would be unfair competition. She was not proud of herself for being down on people; she wanted to think of herself as a big person, magnanimous even, certainly not so petty. But here she was having very small thoughts.

By the time she got home, Jill was anxious to accomplish some work on her new fields before going out dancing. She was tired and she'd have only a little more than an hour or so before heading back to Dano's Dance Inn. She couldn't help thinking what a ridiculous name that was.

Michelle had obviously sensed her friend's ambivalence, because she called her seemingly the minute Jill got in the door.

"Jill, don't back out!" Michelle admonished. "Listen, after this fraking day and Bill's debacle, having a night out with the girls is just what we need."

Jill, still dispirited, sighed.

"Did I tell you that a lot of the guys from the computer processor company near the bar hang out there weekday nights?"

"If you had said *men* instead of *guys,* I might be more interested," Jill grudgingly admitted.

"Good point, but anyway it's time you got out more. Be there. I'm counting on you."

"Okay," Jill said with a lack of conviction. "Bye."

She turned her radio to a country western station to get in the right mood. Still the same old gloomy lyrics to the songs. Still the funny twists. Yet the music was upbeat, despite the mostly mournfully worded messages. Even when the songs were about sadness and crying in their beer there was, somehow, hope within the songs. You knew they would pull through, and Jill decided she would too. She'd go have fun, dance, meet a few interesting guys, and the least that could happen was a fun night out with the girls. What use was whining?

***

Jill found some soon-to-be-expired yogurt in the fridge and threw extra raisins in it for the iron. She went to her home computer and sent off an e-mail to Jason; he'd pick it up on his cell phone. She informed him about what time she'd be home after her night out. She included a subtle reminder to pick up his grandma later by thanking him for his willingness and helpfulness as well as reiterating the approximate agreed-upon time. A second e-mail was sent to the family home day care, letting Fern know that when Jason picked up Stina, Fern should ask him about the adult diapers. Jason's trunk was filled with them, and with him it was out of sight, out of mind. She shuddered to think what would happen if he forgot and opened up his trunk in front of friends to pull out some kind of sports equipment. On further thought, she realized he'd probably just laugh it off, but she would be mortified for him just hearing such a story.

Jill didn't take time to change into her farm work clothes. She just fired up her cultivator and cleared out the middle lavender field. After that satisfying task, she took a shower and actually found a cute outfit to wear. Admittedly, it was a little obvious. The fringe on the jacket sleeves might have been too much. She was beginning to feel better about the evening, though, and vowed to at least try to have some fun.

Michelle met her in the club's parking lot. She looked really cute in her usual riding jeans and cowboy hat, pushed back from her forehead. As they headed into the club, Michelle said, "Your boots, my dear."

She handed Jill the cowboy boots that Jill had worn once before, when riding at Michelle's little ranch. "You should just keep these. They're a little too small for me and a little too big for you. Here." She pulled a pair of thick socks out of her purse. "Put these on too."

Jill changed into the boots at a side table after they'd entered. She felt ridiculous with those thick padded socks. It reminded her of junior high, when she'd had to stuff her bra with tissues. Then she'd found out her fifteen-year-old date had stuffed his shorts with a sock. No wonder they called those dances sock hops. She put her shoes into the same bag that Michelle had given her, and Michelle gave them to a bartender to stash back on a shelf, out of the way. Now with her boots on, she was game. They did look cute, and they made her walk taller. Plus she'd worn her tightest jeans, and everyone had to admit Jill had a great figure—when she allowed herself to show it off.

She took a good look around. The place was noisy, dark, and cool. In one corner a small band was setting up. Live music? That was something Jill hadn't expected and was appreciated. There was also lots of laughter and, as yet, it didn't sound forced or drunken. There was a real wooden bar surround. Jill noticed there were poles here and there along a narrow raised side stage. She caught sight of Lurline, who was waving at them. Michelle went to the microphone to work up the crowd and get them involved in a dancing lesson. Jill was surprised there were more males than females. Immediately, both Jill and Lurline received a lot of attention, which would make it fun while they learned the dance steps.

Lurline ordered nonalcoholic drinks for her and Jill, as she was very fussy about what she put in her body. In fact, although Lurline always brought donuts or something just as convenient to team meetings, Jill never saw her eat one. She knew as much about foods as Cheryl, the hospice nutritionist, did. Lurline's one strict rule was she could eat and drink what she wanted only one day a week.

Jill couldn't believe anybody could really keep true to that rule. Anyway, Jill's rule had evolved into six days a week you felt guilty about eating too much or the wrong things and then on the last day of the week you tried to eat right. That was Jill's average. Admittedly she'd been doing better than that the last few weeks. Because she was so active and now ran a lot, her weight didn't vary. It was her general overall health she was starting to become concerned about. When she'd recently turned forty and found herself in a different world. She actually had aches and pains on occasion, and she had a few gray hairs interspersed with her dark hair. There were too many of them to try and call them highlights. Not to mention she'd need reading glasses soon. After age forty, shit happened. That's all there was to it…not that she hadn't been warned.

Michelle was good with announcing the steps. Her pace was not too fast but not too slow, and her voice kept up with the beat of the music. Jill did turn the wrong way a few times, once almost smacking into one of the poles, and the last mistake made her bump into a pretty good-looking guy who laughed with her.

Toward the end of the lesson, Lane arrived. Her blonde hair was curled and worn long. She was dressed in high strapped sandals and had on a low-cut blouse…very low. Though the cleavage wasn't that noticeable in comparison to her provocative shorts, which were the shortest shorts Jill had ever seen. That girl was beautiful. It seemed most everyone came to that conclusion, because she immediately had three guys surrounding her.

After the lesson, the four of them found a table. Michelle seemed to know everyone by name. It was easy for the guys to see she was the real thing—a real cowgirl. This obvious genuineness was attracting the few legitimate cowboys present. Several of the wannabe cowboys were hanging around too. The computer sales and manufacturing moguls were all over Lane. Already, two guys were vying to be the first to dance with her.

Jill dug out her journal from her purse where it was stashed under the table and decided to keep it near her to write down a few of her impressions during the evening.

When the two of them were left alone after the Michelle's admirers followed her to the bar, Lurline told Jill, "Don't you worry. Lane will skim off all the superficial guys, the ones who care only about youth and looks, and we'll wait for the real McCoys."

They waited.

Jill was about to order a bona fide drink when a man who limped approached her. Strange, she'd just seen him dancing away without any physical problems.

"Looks like a Hatfield heading this way," Lurline said.

He extended his hand to Jill. Curious, she accepted his offer to dance. Sure enough the minute they started dancing, the limp went away. What was that about? After the lively dance, he limped all the way back while taking Jill to her table. Lurline was chewing on ice and squeezing lime slices into her drink. Lane and Michelle were back at the table too. Taking a break, they said. Jill explained that the guy had told her that when he's dancing he felt no pain. He'd said that dancing was a cure-all.

Jill remembered, and told her co-workers now that they were all at the same table, that a patient's wife had recently told her that dancing was better than sex.

"He'd have to be a really good dancer," Michelle stated.

"A professional even," Lurline added. Soon they were all laughing together.

During a short lull in the conversation, Lane now returned to the table, asked the rest of them if they'd heard the phrase *dirt nap*.

Michal Poe

"Sure," everyone at the table offered.

Lane explained that today, her patient's son had said that. She didn't even understand what it meant at first. "Doesn't seem a very reverent way to talk about your elderly father's death," she said.

"The one I hate is *joining the majority*," Lurline stated. "If I hear that one more time…"

"*I don't like, giving up the ghost*. And I deplore *they earned their angel wings*," Jill said. "Who decided people turn into angels?"

"I've heard that. That's kind of pretty," Lane said. "There's another one too. I forget. You guys will think of it. I kinda liked it."

"Was it *buying the farm*?" Michelle asked. "That's my personal dislike. That, as well as *kicking the bucket*. I don't understand that image at all."

"Oh, I remember that other one, my uncle said it—*Go to sleep with the Tribbles*. It's some kind of sci-fi thing he saw in a chat room, because he's online all the time." Lane said.

"Donna's husband? He's online all the time?" Lurline asked, knowing full well it was none of her business. Although everyone knew Lane was Donna's niece, it wasn't spoken about in the office. Certainly, Donna seldom mentioned her spouse. Kim had met him and she'd been very quiet about relaying any information to the rest of the team. They did know the man was disabled somehow, and that he was a good cook.

Lane didn't answer Lurline's question. She looked away over to the dance floor, apparently pretending not to hear that inquiry and tapping one of her sandals in beat with the music.

Jill broke the slight awkwardness in the exchange. "Remember that doctor who always said, *circling the drain*? Colorful and picturesque, but wrong!" Jill exclaimed.

"Another guy said, '*time to croak.*' At least I understood what he meant," Lane said, joining in the conversation again before being whisked off for another dance.

Jill picked up her journal again. "Keep talking," she said, "I'm writing these all down."

Michelle and Lurline had fun taking turns shouting out all the rest of the various terms they'd heard for death or dying. Jill wrote down the unusual ones. She liked *sweet chariot ride,* and *paying the final forward.*

Then Jill remembered a few more. "I just heard *the last exit* this week. You know in the hospital where I first worked, they always put "*ceased to breathe*" on the charts. Or they would announce over the intercom, "Dr. So and So, we have an expected *CTB.*"

"How about *going in*? That one I heard from a pilot…I once dated," Lurline concluded.

Lurline's last line took the steam out of that little game. It had been fun for a while. Still there wasn't too much dancing. Lurline fanned herself a few times with her napkin. Her action could be mistaken for having a hot flash. She seemed to realize that wouldn't bring anyone around. Jill noticed that she was undoing a few of the top buttons on her blouse.

"Oh, no you don't," Jill joked. She knew Lurline always wore a sports bra under her clothes. She was adamant about it. She said not only did it fight the ravages of gravity, it could reverse it. Jill sincerely doubted that last part.

Michelle got up and headed out to lead another dance. On her way, she pointed out to Jill and Lurline that it looked as if Dano, the club owner, was heading for their table. Dano nodded to Michelle as he passed by her. He took the chair next to Jill. Michelle raised her eyebrows and gave Jill a knowing smile from halfway across the room.

"Hello," Dano said. Then he asked, "Could I ask you ladies what you do for a living?"

"You can ask," Lurline answered. "But why do you need to know?"

"It's just that a few of the married men here came to me and were a little concerned about a couple of ladies they thought were private eyes or something. They told me that these women weren't doing much dancing, mostly just talking. They really became alarmed they said, when it appeared that one of them was taking notes."

Jill and Lurline laughed.

Lurline explained, "We work in health care and we're writing down interesting phrases." Then she added in a little more subdued manner, "The reason we're not dancing much is because nobody's even asking."

That last part sounded pathetic.

Still, Dano laughed. "Well," he said, "Those same guys were attracted, even if you were working for a divorce lawyer. But then they noticed you two weren't drinking. That scared them too."

"We don't need to attract the married men," Lurline said.

"I'm single," Dano said, looking right at Jill.

Jill felt a little flustered, yet emboldened. She said, "May I ask you a question?"

"Sure."

"Why are these poles everywhere?" She asked as she pointed in their direction along the periphery.

"Huh? Oh, the poles. I'm Italian. This used to be a titty bar, but I cleaned it up. You know, adjust to whatever milieu you end up in. Cowboys are easy. How about you cowgirls?"

"We're not easy," Lurline said, "And honestly, we're not cowgirls."

"Fair enough," Dano said. "What're you ladies drinking? I'll get another for you."

"Seltzer and lime, extra lime." Lurline answered.

Smiling, Dano left the table.

Jill and Lurline looked at one another. The music was loud, the beat was good, and there they sat.

Michelle, having finished her dance and on the way back to the table, was intercepted by Dano. They stood talking for a few minutes.

"Jeez," Jill said, "I hope we didn't get her in trouble. Is it time to go home, Lurline?" she asked, suddenly feeling tired and old.

"I notice the younger crowd leaving and the more regular type, older guys filtering in," Lurline said, sounding a little hopeful. "It's starting to look more promising. Let's stay a little longer."

Michelle came back to the table. "Wow, you guys impressed Dano. He wanted to ask one of you to dance, but he said you looked a little intimidating."

"Oh, brother." Jill said. "What next: if you're not easy, you're intimidating?"

"Cowboys work hard all day. They don't like to work for their women. It's all yes or no. Nothing in between," Michelle explained.

"If Dano is a cowboy, I'm a princess," Lurline said.

"It's so simple, it's complicated," Michelle offered.

Jill added, "Come to think of it, it did sound that way on the country western station."

"Let 'em pay then, if they don't like to put in a little effort," Lurline said. "And what's Dano handing out all the time?"

"Condoms," Michelle answered. "He likes everybody to practice safe sex."

"I don't want anybody who just practices," Lurline asserted.

"Hey look, Lane is taking a break. You two, are you sure you guys wouldn't want a beer or something to kind of cheer you up?" Michelle asked.

Neither Jill nor Lurline wanted to have to have a drink just to cheer up.

Lane sat down and spread her long legs in front of her, lacing the sandals she'd kicked off earlier. "Listen, friends," she said when she'd finished, "I'm gonna leave now. An older crowd is moving in, and it doesn't look promising. They look 'like they've been rode hard and put away wet.' Oh, that saying is so funny." She giggled. "That tall guy, Lyle just told me that. He also said he likes you, Michelle. He said you guys used to have a thing."

"He had a thing. I had no-thing," Michelle said in answer.

Lane touched up her lipstick, pushed a stray curl behind her ear, and continued, "Thanks for a fun evening. We should do this every Wednesday night." With that she sashayed out. Just about every eye was on her cellulite-free butt cheeks peeking out beneath her short shorts.

Now Jill was ready. She ordered a beer, just to set on the table, if nothing else. Lurline glared at her and squeezed more lime sections into her seltzer.

Michelle was emphatic about them staying put. "Well, now we know the problem: they thought you guys were trouble."

"I see," Jill said. "Apparently they weren't drunk enough yet to purposely walk into trouble."

Michelle ignored that comment. "You know, I'll send a few guys over with more patience. The kind of trait you develop when working with animals and wresting a living from the land."

Lurline about choked on her lime wedge.

Soon, two fairly good-looking and interesting guys joined them. They knew Michelle too. They loved to dance, were real cowboys, were single (Michelle could attest), and had the advantage of not frantically needing to lay someone every night.

The evening picked up. They had fun. Michelle was in her element. She even sat on the drummer's lap and kept the beat through most of one song, until she accidentally fell off. This caused a lot more laughter, since she wasn't hurt. So Jill danced and the little group at the table talked and even philosophized. It was the deeper kind of talk that the alcohol brought out in the guys. The topics discussed seemed important at the time, but Jill knew that the next day, in retrospect, the conversation wouldn't sound as profound.

Jill noticed Dano looking at her quite a bit. But it seemed he was he also trying to catch Lurline's eye. Jill found herself flirting with him. She'd noticed the smell of cigars on him when he'd sat next to her earlier. That was interesting. She hated smoking, but cigars, that was different. They brought back memories of sitting under the table and listening to her beloved grandpa and some of his friends talk and play pinochle. Sometimes the air would be almost blue from her grandfather's cigar smoke, which always hung in the air at his lake cottage.

She and Lurline ended up admitting they were having fun. But as eleven got closer to twelve o'clock, they knew it was time to go home. It was a weekday night after all. Jill drove home with her boots on. She was really becoming very fond of them. They did make her seem taller.

After she got home, she had reason to be very upset. All was quiet there, but Jill noticed a paper burger joint hat on the kitchen table next to Jason's car keys along with a bag of change marked TIPS. She had a suspicion that these things belonged to Jason, and they added up to a part-time afternoon job. It appeared that after all their talk he'd gone ahead and gotten a job anyway. He knew this issue had not been solved and Jill specifically did not approve. The dilemma was how to call out her sweet, obviously ambitious son and call him to task for getting a job.

Rather than act rashly and go wake him up, Jill decided she'd have to think on this, sleep on it. She was tired. She checked in on her mom and went to bed.

***

THURSDAY

The next morning, Jill woke rested, so she got up very early to take a short run. After her shower she noticed the kitchen table was now cleared of last night's items. Jason.

She dressed her mom and sat her down with her oatmeal. Stina was usually more alert in the morning and remembered how to eat and hold a spoon too. Sometimes she would reach down, put her face in the food, and eat it that way. Jill didn't mind. It was sad, but when it came to her mother, Jill was used to sad. She had begun to teach herself to treasure the small moments with her mother. Especially the times when she looked into her mom's eyes and saw the real Stina. At those times she would hug her mom, smooth down her hair, and say, "It'll be all right." Those same words Stina had used with Jill so many times during Jill's life.

Jason came down for breakfast. He drank his morning orange juice, draining a full quart right from the carton. Then he cleared his throat.

With his back to her and while putting the carton back in the fridge, he said, "Mom, I know you probably know I got an afternoon job." He turned toward her as he shut the fridge. "It's just two or three hours, most weekdays. The opportunity came up suddenly and I just took it. Are you mad?"

"I was upset last night, Jason." She took the empty carton out of the fridge and threw it in the trash. "I don't know why this has been such an issue with me. I guess that since I had to struggle and earn my own way, I wanted it easier for you. You are so much help with Mom too, I think part of my reasoning was selfish."

"Uh-huh," Jason said.

He was learning her tricks. She tried to express her feelings. "The worst thing to me is having you do it without telling me about it. It makes me feel as if you don't trust me; that hurts."

"That was way wrong. I'm sorry."

As usual, Jill's heart immediately thawed. She went to Jason and messed up his hair—a very annoying gesture on her part, but Jason knew what it meant.

***

Thursdays were usually hectic. There was always so much to do in the week, and on Thursdays the staff realized that there were only two more weekdays to accomplish all their work Jill had no reason to think today would be any different. Especially since when she arrived at work, right on time, she found most everyone else already there, talking about Bill's fiasco on the news.

Ron stopped her before she even got to her desk. "Donna's in there with Bill again. No yelling this time though."

"I hope this turns out alright. Poor Donna, she probably didn't get a wink of sleep last night."

Ron and Jill hunkered down to get their day organized. After a while Ron spoke. "Jill, last night I saw Melissa Sanchez and her husband at their son Raul's soccer game."

"Oh, that's wonderful."

"Yeah, Tammy and I were taking Jake to his little league practice and they were just finishing up the soccer junior finals. Melissa looked good. Her husband recognized me.

He said that Melissa agreed to get out of the house in her wheelchair more often now that she'd found out she could do something with her hair."

"It was something so simple. Jangles helped too."

"He was very grateful, Jill. He said to thank you again."

"Hmm," Jill said as she continued her work. "Good. That was a fun and very satisfying visit."

Kim walked by, coming from Dean's office. She had a large folder stuffed full of clippings and a few fell out near Ron.

"You dropped some junk, Kim," he said.

"Oh, of all the days. I need this stuff though," Kim lamented as she began to pick up the various scraps of paper. "Everybody's in such a sour mood that nobody can think of any jokes for me."

"What am I missing?" Jill asked.

"It's that roast at three-thirty. I need good jokes."

"A roast?" Ron asked.

"People, I already told you about it. Remember? Instead of a regular funeral, all Shane's friends are going to come and do a comedy roast on him. There's a good lineup of speakers—you know, old comic friends of his. Mrs. Shane said more than a few have even come up from LA."

"That's what he wanted?"

"Absolutely. His wife, I mean widow, is very excited about the whole thing. I have to emcee. I'm not good at jokes, not intentional ones anyway," she added with a little laugh. "I did just get one from Dean. 'How many grieving people does it take to change a light bulb? Ha, ha, none, because they need to sit in the dark.'"

"That's not very funny," Sandy said.

Michal Poe

"I know," Kim admitted. "I'm looking for upbeat jokes or nice put-down jokes. Like what's his name, you know, Bob Newhart's best friend."

"Don Rickles?" Ron asked, "That's what you call nice put-downs?"

"Bob Newhart," Sandy said, adding, "What century are you from?"

Kim replied, "I need people who at least remember the last century."

"Maybe some of Bill Cosby's jokes," Jill suggested.

"Is he still funny?" Ron asked. "Anyway, Kim, don't you have any connections?"

"I used to, but they've all died. The new ones only know jokes with all that questionable language."

"It's a roast! But I guess the fact they're giving it for a dead man is questionable enough," Ron stated.

Lane came into the office, surprised to find everybody still in the workroom. "Team should already be started. What are you all doing in here?" she asked.

"Waiting for you," Sandy quipped.

Kim sighed. "Let's just go and get this over with."

Only Dr. Almerst was sitting at the conference table. He had a saucer next to him with a few pita chips and a strawberry. Not his usual loaded plate. He looked a little pensive. Lurline had washed off the side table and was arranging an array of food. Concentrically arranged on a large black ceramic plate were little squares of green things with dark green mint leaves on top. Next to that was a small platter of toasted pita-bread wedges with a delicious-smelling bowl of hummus. Behind those were several artistic vegetable scenarios. Especially enticing were the mini-croissants with dark chocolate oozing out their edges and a beautiful plate of strawberries with almond sliver stems. Real crystal glasses sat next to a carafe of fresh-squeezed orange juice. There was even a silver tea set and an espresso machine.

All the workers noted the scrumptious-looking items, now marvelously laid out on a linen tablecloth.

"This is beautiful!" Kim exclaimed.

"Wow, what's the occasion?" Jill asked.

"Oh, you know how my wife Sharon likes to do things. She was up at four-thirty grinding garbanzos. Food is her art," Dr. Almerst answered.

Jill felt the need to give the doctor some appreciation. She went up to him and gave him a hug. "You're always so helpful to all of us, Stan. Sometimes we forget to thank you." Stan gave an almost shy smile. Jill could tell he was pleased.

Everyone got a plate and loaded up. They figured they would need the sustenance. Jill really liked the espresso machine. Ron knew how to use it.

"Yes," he said, "I was a barista, once. Except it wasn't called that then. The best thing I did there was meet my wife."

They had settled in and were about to start on their patient list when Donna and Bill came into the conference room through Bill's private door. A rather subdued, bowed but not broken, Bill made one of his usual, hard-to-take comments.

"Shouldn't you wait for the host before you start the party?" he said, while eyeing the prodigious amounts of food on everyone's plates.

No one answered.

Donna looked at the side table and said, "Stan, tell your wife thanks for all her work. Bill, would you like something?"

Michal Poe

"After, yes…after. Now, staff, before we begin, you must remember to stay for a few minutes after team as our nutritionist, whose office is in team B's facility, will be here to review the nutritional supplements that are now on the market." He continued in his most grandiloquent manner, "As an aside, that interview last evening didn't go exactly as planned…I don't know whether any of you saw it…but that vets guy was very volatile and the host was simply rude. I did my best to get our good name out there, but didn't entirely succeed. Donna, however, will appear on another station this Friday, I believe, and represent the hospice consortium. So let's give Donna a hand for setting this up so quickly."

He stood and began clapping. Those seated politely clapped as well, while breathing a sigh of relief to know that Donna would have a chance to rectify things. Donna's face was turned toward the wall as she was dishing up her plate, so no one could read her expression. When she sat, she had her usual calm demeanor and the workers were able to relax a little as they chewed their way through the patient review.

It was difficult, as they had to divide Ron's patients for the next week, and as Jill had expected and discussed previously with Ron, it was a sure thing that Jill was getting all the difficult cases. Even at that, Lane complained about doing more first visits. Bill reminded her that she would get the extra points and wouldn't have to continue on as case manager on all of those new people. He then commended the staff for turning in their production sheets and announced the tally would be made on Friday.

Jill reported she was to see the Sealys again, to follow up on the cleanup. Thankfully, Sandy didn't go into detail about the animal farce. Jill also let the team know her concerns about Mary Bonsine, who was a fairly new patient and hadn't been previously discussed at length. Jill stated Mary was refusing visits, and Jill suspected she might need more help for her care to remain in the home setting. She also let the staff know the appointment was set up with all the Dobson family to ask about the possibility of getting a better schedule. It was hard to keep current as to where to find him. Jill asked Lurline to see Roger and Randy at Hope House and set up their surroundings so that Randy could get out a little more. Lurline said she could also help rearrange the area around the hospital bed and bring out an organizer that would allow him to better keep tabs on all his medicines.

Michelle reported she had some extra time this week, if anyone else needed her. She revealed that she and Jill would visit the Coultans together on Friday to see if they could get some honest communication going between the couple and get some help for the spouse. Michelle emphasized to the team that the couple's long history of marital disagreements would probably continue. She advised any staff visiting to only attend to his hospice-related concerns to avoid being drawn into a black hole of bickering.

"The vortex of vehemence," Jill volunteered. Bill gave her a quick look. Jill caught herself in time and was able to stop herself from calling out another phrase. Instead, she decided she would concentrate on jokes for Kim. It did appear that no one, aside from that look from Bill, had paid any attention to her remark. Except she then noticed Dean giving her a knowing smile. She figured he too had been in a pit of pettiness. Jill wondered if she would write these phrases in her journal. Why not? She kept it just for her own mental health. It might be good to write more rather than speak out in team. It was irritating enough to get any "look" from Bill. She didn't need to get one for being trite.

Ron explained that their long-time patient James Speil was graduating from hospice as, amazingly, his illnesses had been steadily improving. The last several visits Ron had made to the patient showed normal-sounding lungs, and all his standard lab work was unremarkable.

Ron reviewed his notes saying, "Speil's doctor revealed that the cancer is somewhat cleared, very stable, and his heart problems are resolving as well." Ron reminded the staff, "Do you remember him? He was the guy who got the phrase *DO NOT REVIVE* tattooed on his chest to avoid being resuscitated."

"He's that much better?" Jill queried. Then she added, "That's wonderful."

"Wonderful, except," Ron continued, "When I went to the home to get James to sign the hospice revocation form, James said he wanted hospice to pay for the laser tattoo removal, since he wasn't terminal after all."

"No. Absolutely not," Bill bellowed. "It's not our fault if our patients get well."

Sandy, true to form, yelled out, "Tell him to just keep his shirt on!" That broke the tension and the rest of the meeting went well, as did the short presentation by the nutritionist, Cheryl Yee.

Cheryl was a good speaker. She appeared pulling a cart laden with sample products. She was quick, precise, and knowledgeable. She was unquestionably overweight, but appeared, as she herself said, "fit and fat." She gave all the nurses several samples of canned nutritional supplements and new recipes for homemade, high-calorie shakes. She was pleased to say there were many new products for diabetics, children, those who were lactose intolerant, soy avoiders, and those who needed fiber enrichment. Jill received a whole case, plus a few six-packs filled with various flavors. It was more stuff to keep in the back of her Jeep, but she was pleased to have them. Her patients always complained they had to buy a set amount and then find out they hated the product. This way she could give them a sample of the various types and flavors.

Back in the workroom, Jill was anxious to get out and see her patients. But her workbag was a mess, and she needed to organize her day. She started to make her appointments, halfway listening to the conversations around her.

She heard Donna tell Lurline that she'd called the VA first thing and found out the name of Chambers' boss. She'd then called her and mentioned that Community Hospice wished to make a contribution to the vets' combat-related PTSD fund, since so many of the Community Hospice patients had used their counsel. Dean had given her that idea, she said, and it was very useful. She said the local news station had called her early in the morning at her home.

"It seems Bill gave them my number and said I was in charge of public relations," Donna chuckled. "I guess I am. Anyway, thank heavens he thought to do that rather than talk to them himself. That's when they decided upon a talk about the consortium of hospice providers, thinking it would be a good program in itself. I'm assigned to set up a panel."

Lurline shook her head in amazement. "That was genius."

"Dean's suggestion was germinal and probably a bit manipulative, but not illegal."

Michal Poe

Ron looked at Jill, as he'd been listening as well. They both smiled, knowing they were in good hands.

Kim stood up from her desk chair and loudly beseeched the group to come up with more jokes.

"Here's one," Ron said. "The doctor said, 'Mr. Shane, you only have one night left to live. Do whatever you want.' So when he gets home he tells his wife what the doctor said. 'Honey, I want to make love all night.' Then she says, 'Oh, no, you don't, I'll be exhausted the next morning, and I'll be the only one who has to get up again.'"

"That is wrong on so many levels," Michelle said. "Although that would be perfect for the Coultans."

"Thanks, Ron," Kim said, "I may use it, although I bet one of the other comics already has that one covered."

"They really want that kind of humor?" Dean questioned as he and Sandy were arranging all the extra supplement cans the nutritionist had left on the conference table into the supply shelving area.

"Yep, they do," Kim answered.

"My grandpop," Lurline glanced quickly heavenward, "Always said that once he got old almost everything hurt, and what didn't hurt wouldn't work."

"I saw that joke once. Did he get it off the Internet?" Lane asked.

Lurline sighed, "There was no Internet when my grandfather was alive."

Jill, finishing her own patient scheduling appointments for the day, walked over to Kim to say, "It's possible that I might be able to come to the funeral."

Kim looked very relieved. "Mrs. Shane would like that."

"Here's a joke if Shane played poker," Jill said.

"He did. Some of those guys will be there too."

"Okay." Jill explained, "My new patient, Mr. Goulden, is giving a memorial for his dad at Pansy's Card Room on Saturday night. I don't know how to word it, but he said something like, 'I know my daddy's in poker heaven because God finally called his bluff.'"

Kim laughed, "That's good."

Ron suddenly grabbed his bag and was rushing out of the office.

"Ron," Jill called, "You forgot your folders."

"Oh, darn it. Thanks Jill," he said as he quickly retrieved his paperwork. "Oh yeah, you were gonna see this guy with me. When do you think you could come by? Though I might call you for advice even before you could get there. I just got a call from Chase's mother. She said her son was under a bush in the yard, was there most of the night, and she needs me right now."

Jill moaned. "Under a bush? Oh, God. What a way to start Thursday."

***

Jill left the office later than she wanted. But since Ron was to do the bulk of the visit with his young patient, Chase Miller, her day wasn't overly scheduled.

Unfortunately, when she arrived at the Millers' things were in an upheaval. No one answered the doorbell, so she walked through the side gate. Chase was still under one of the bushes on the far side of the yard, near the swimming pool. It appeared as if he was in or on a sleeping bag, but he was way back against the fence. Jill assumed those were his feet barely sticking out. Ron was sitting on the ground near the bush.

Chase's parents stood nearby. His mother saw Jill and ran to her, exclaiming in a loud, high voice, "Are you the nurse who'll be here next week? We should put Chase in a hospital so he can't escape!"

Ron said, in a normal tone of voice but loud enough for her to hear, "Mrs. Miller, he's just in his own backyard. You know he likes fresh air."

"I suppose it's okay for him to die under a bush!" Mrs. Miller hysterically exclaimed.

"Let Ron talk," Mr. Miller firmly commanded.

Ron got up and walked over to the trio. "We've talked, and Chase told me what he wants. We need everyone's help in order for him to do it."

Mr. Miller put his arm around his wife, holding her rather tightly. "What is it? Whatever it is, we'll do it, if it's humanly possible."

Mrs. Miller frowned and tried to wiggle out of her husband's embrace. But he held her arm and looked into her eyes as he spoke. "Honey, we need to honor his wishes. His life is…" there was a catch in his throat, "…is so short."

"He just wants to go camping one more time." Ron said.

"No, not in his condition!" Mrs. Miller exclaimed.

"Well, I agree with that. He's too weak," Ron said.

"See?" Mrs. Miller emphasized.

Jill stood by, watching Ron work.

Ron continued, "Chase knows he's too weak, so he's come up with a good compromise. His best buddy is in town, and a few of the guys want to pitch a tent here and have a campfire. Then they'll sleep out under the stars. It's a small thing, but important for Chase."

"That's all?" Mr. Miller asked. "Yes, we'll do it. He can do that. Thank you, thank you." He went over to the bush and, speaking in the direction of his son, said, "I'm going to get all the camping gear and throw it back here. You'll have a good time, Chase. Invite your friends. This is a good idea. I love you, son."

From beneath the bush, they heard Chase. "Okay, dad. Help me out, please."

Ron and Mr. Miller helped Chase out and up, which took some effort as he needed total support. Meanwhile Jill talked quietly with his mother about her son. Mrs. Miller was now contrite and tearful, but her voice was strained. Jill ascertained that the sicker Chase became, the more overprotective his mom felt.

"Jill I want him to go to bed and lie very still, and then maybe he'll live longer. My husband told me that doesn't make sense; in fact he told me it was dead wrong."

After a brief pause, Mrs. Miller began to wring her hands. She looked right into Jill's eyes, and Jill felt the woman's distress as she continued, "I know he wants to live as fully as he can before he dies, but isn't that going to rush things? I want to do what is best for him. I love him."

"I see that, Mrs. Miller. Anyone can see how much you love him."

Mrs. Miller looked up at Jill with big tears in her eyes. "Jill, do you think I'm wrong?"

"It's not wrong for you to feel that way. But sometimes we have to pull back and see the bigger picture."

"What do you mean?"

"Chase wants to feel more independent, more in charge of his life, during the time he has left. There's a balance there somewhere, don't you think?"

Michal Poe

"So you don't agree with me; that his using his energy for this stuff is giving up, or reckless. It won't shorten his life?"

"I honestly don't know," Jill said as she took Mrs. Miller's arm and gently guided her over toward a patio chair. Now sitting and facing her, Jill added, "Maybe it will shorten his life by a few days or even a week. But the quality of the time he has left, that's the most important thing for him, not just the length of it."

Mrs. Miller had stopped wringing her hands and now sat very still on her rattan chair across from Jill. She sat looking at her hands for a while and then looked over across the pool where Ron, her husband, and Chase sat talking.

Jill softly asked, "What do you really think? Imagine yourself in Chase's place. Can you?"

Mrs. Miller now spoke in a normal voice. "He always was a fun person. He always had a lot of friends. Maybe I don't have to give up on him; maybe just give in a little. Is that what you mean by balance?"

"Uh-huh," Jill answered.

They sat there for a while listening to the men across the way. They even heard some laughter. The sounds were pleasant. Jill noted how much pleasure Mrs. Miller took in hearing her son laugh.

After a little while, Mrs. Miller smiled. "Thank you. I guess I just needed someone to talk to."

"Yes, I think you're right," Jill said. "I'll be filling in for Ron next week and I'll save some extra time for you. Would you review the services we offer in that hospice booklet too? When you have time, you might benefit from a group or having the social worker come out to listen. Whatever you think is best."

Mrs. Miller stood up, "I'm going to go over there and see what they're up to now. Thank you, Jill."

"Okay," Jill said. "See you next week."

Jill let herself out. She made a quick note to discuss ideas with Michelle about what pre-bereavement group might be right for Mrs. Miller. Everyone always said losing a child was the hardest thing. From her own experience, Jill thought that might be true. Your child might be six or sixty, but still…your child.

One the way to the Bonsines' house, she continued to think about the way Ron had handled things. She was very impressed. She reflected on the fact that Ron took everything in stride. This was one of his best qualities. His comment about Mrs. Miller, back at the office, bothered her a bit though. He'd said, "She's impossible." But Jill knew Mrs. Miller wasn't impossible. True, it was an impossible situation. With her son coming up to Chase's age, Jill didn't know if she could handle it any differently herself. She realized Ron hadn't had the time to have a good talk with Mrs. Miller before. Maybe they should always go out in teams of two. It was so reassuring for the patients and the staff too.

***

Jill took a shortcut to her next patient. Lane had opened Mary Bonsine two weeks ago. Jill had seen her only once since. Jill was concerned about her living situation, and she decided that she would try to be extra observant today and see if there was anything else she could do for Mary.

After driving to an industrial area near the airport, she noted Mary's little cement block house connected to a larger building in the back. It was a strange configuration. Jill sat in her Jeep for a few minutes, looking over Mary's chart, then she headed up to the entrance. She stood waiting at the door while someone inside opened several locks. She heard very loud noises and remembered that same commotion the last time she'd visited. It sounded like a lot of grinding and clunking from the fenced-off courtyard of the building behind. With the continuous racket, how could her patient get any rest?

Jill began to think about all of her patients many complaints regarding their hospital visits. The one they all reported was the raucous and continuous commotion. Mainly, they hated the noise. Jill was of an old-fashioned school of thought. Quiet, calm surroundings were important for healing. That was the last thing you got in a hospital environment or, for that matter, any institutional environment. When one of the hospice patients had to be admitted to the hospital for some reason, Jill and the other nurses had made up some signs to be placed on the doors, or near the beds. "Quiet zone," one said. "Extra need for rest," said another. Jill had never seen those requests honored. Once you entered the hospital machine, you were duly processed. Many of the interruptions to the patients were procedures needed for the safety of the patient and the hospital personnel. But it made for an unpleasant stay. Most of the hospice patients' first plea to the nurses when they went out to the home to open the patient to home services was, please don't ever make me go back to the hospital again.

Her attention was brought back to the Bonsine home. She heard someone inside, swearing about all the locks on the door. It was taking a long, long time. She went back to her thoughts. She had given birth to Jason in the hospital.

She had wanted a home delivery from a midwife, but it was her first child, and her husband Chris was absolutely terrified of the idea. She gave birth very late in the day and stayed one night in the hospital. An aide had awakened her, stating that the nurse would be coming by with a sleeping pill if she needed it. Jill thought, but didn't answer in a sarcastic way, *"Well, I guess I'll need it now."* She'd later realized, with all the hospital noise, she could have used two.

"Hello. Sorry it took me so long to get the damned door open," Mr. Bonsine apologized. He was totally out of breath and doubled over from the effort. "I didn't get much sleep last night; I might doze off while you're here." He slowly began to limp back over to his chair.

"Don't worry, Mr. Bonsine," Jill said, smiling, "I'll wake you if I need you. How's Mary?" she asked of his back.

"She's right here." He motioned toward the back wall, saying, "Mary, your nurse is here." This effort started Mr. Bonsine coughing.

Jill could see how short of breath and pale he was. She recognized his cough as an unproductive hacking, and it didn't bode well. "Mr. Bonsine, may I make a doctor's appointment for you? I don't like the sound of that cough. I'll bet your doctor wouldn't like it either."

Mr. Bonsine answered gruffly between coughs. "I'm not going anywhere."

Jill sighed. It was his right. But he didn't sound well. "You call me if you change your mind and need help getting a quicker appointment, okay?" She was not his assigned nurse, so she could only offer.

It was very dark in the almost windowless room. Jill's eyes adjusted, and she spied Mary lying in a hospital bed that was pushed up against the wall. Mary looked up with sleepy eyes when Jill approached.

"Mary, do you mind if I open the curtains and the blinds a bit?" Jill asked. "I can barely see you, and I know I won't be able to find what I need in my bag."

"No, no!" Mary exclaimed very quickly. "My son, Jerome, he doesn't allow the curtains opened. He says it disturbs his workers."

"It does?" She realized Mary's comment didn't make any sense. But hearing the urgency in Mary's voice, Jill soothed her by saying, "Don't worry, Mary, I'll use my flashlight again."

Jill saw that Mr. Bonsine was already asleep in his recliner, snoring loudly.

"Can you help me up?" Mary asked. "I think I forgot my anti-nausea pill. I can't keep anything straight around here, don't remember much of anything anymore. I need to get that medicine and go to the bathroom before you start poking around on me. I already feel sick."

Jill helped Mary up. Mary, using her walker, and at a snail's pace, headed toward the bathroom through a small kitchenette area.

Jill set out her nursing pad on a side table and pulled out her hand gel to wash up. As soon as Mary was around the corner, out of sight, Jill sidled over to the little window nearest her. She peeked through the heavy, dusty drapes and bent down one of the blind slats. Jill saw that over a partially blocked fence were two large SUVs that were being rapidly stripped of most everything attachable. There was crew of five or six young-looking, buff men. Behind them, Jill saw a big transport truck with signage saying, "Blaston's Refrigerated Meats, Athens, Georgia." Because Jill was good with numbers, she was able to quickly memorize the license plate information as well. Jill quietly let the drape back down. She wasn't sure what she saw, but it didn't look right. She wrote the information in small letters on the cover of Mary's chart, which she pulled out of her bag. In larger letters, she also wrote, "Hospice worker may need escort if patient needs night visit."

After a good assessment on Mary, Jill felt better. She had been able to get many of Mary's symptoms under control. Mary had her medicines totally confused, and it was no wonder she was nauseous. Jill managed to organize Mary's medicine into a regimen she thought she might be able to follow.

Then, right in front of Jill, Mary began to fuss with the medicines again and confused them.

Jill redid them, re-explaining how to use the medicine organizer. She then straightened up the room and put clean linen on Mary's bed, while reviewing services. Mary said she wouldn't let the bathing aide come out, even though it would be useful for her. Also, when Jill suggested a volunteer, she told Jill that no one would be allowed to help her or go pick up her medicines at the pharmacy.

"Thanks for all you do, Jill. Don't worry, I'll be just fine. I get around with my walker, and we don't eat much anyway. I can't expect my husband to help, as you can see. He sleeps all day and night." She laughed ruefully as she nodded toward the recliner.

Mr. Bonsine's snoring now had occasional totally silent lapses, which were a sure sign of sleep apnea. Jill knew that certainly was one of the reasons he was so tired all the time.

"You live here with your son, right? Is he able to help you two?" Jill asked.

Michal Poe

"Jerome? Oh no, he's much too busy, day and night, always working. He shops for us sometimes, but we don't like the stuff he gets, you know corn chips and things. Too hard with the dentures."

"But a volunteer could…"

Jill didn't get a chance to finish as Mary jumped right in with some alarm in her voice, "I said, I told everybody he'd never allow that."

Having read her chart, Jill was able to ask, "Your daughter, then?" in a very calm and matter-of-fact tone.

"She has children. I never get to see her. She refuses to come with him here." She motioned toward the side window. "Jerome has all those young men to supervise."

"Mary," Jill said softly, "I have to ask you. Do you feel safe here? Are you really all right?"

"Oh, yes. The problem is just me. I'm so forgetful. And my husband, well, you see he's not in the best shape himself. Stubborn too, doesn't want any changes."

Jill didn't talk. She waited. Just as she thought, Mary needed a little more time to get her thoughts in order.

"You know, I love my son very much; he's always lived with us. Jerome has some behavior problems, but he's never hurt us. The three of us have been so close. I don't know if I'd ever want anything different."

Jill came closer to Mary when she saw Mary becoming distressed. She went over and put her arm around Mary's shoulders. "Mary, I can come by everyday for a few days and see what else I can do to get you better situated here. I need to know what I can do to help you."

"You're doing good, Jill. Really, we're fine. This is the way it's always been."

Jill sighed. She knew her hands might be tied in trying to get things better situated. There was a fine line between caring and meddling. "I know one thing I can do right now though, Mary. I've got plenty of liquid nutritional supplement samples in my Jeep. I'll bring a few back in for you."

"Okay," Mary said, relaxing a bit. "That would be good, maybe even some for my husband? I guess that will be okay."

Jill unlocked the one lock she'd previously relocked and let herself out. While Jill was getting things from her Jeep, a burly man came in through the side entrance. Jill could see him out of her peripheral vision. Then, as she came closer to the front door with sample cans of supplement, she overheard the conversation. She heard it all clearly because the son was so loud. He probably had a hearing problem working around all that noise.

Now inside, he asked his mother, "Is that bitch going anytime soon?"

"She went to the car to get me something," Mary answered.

"Tell her she can only come once a week. This is not Grand Central Station. Don't make me put you and dad in the nursing home grandpa died in." He slammed the side door on his way back to his work.

Jill was aghast. So this is what was keeping Mary put. On the one hand, she was so mad she was thinking, okay this man is going down, but the other more rational side only told her, You'll need to follow up on this. She approached the front door, which she'd left ajar.

"I'm back with the goods," Jill said, keeping her voice light.

Michal Poe

"Thanks, Jill," Mary said, sounding a little strained. "Just leave them outside the door there. My son will get them, and I'll see you next week. We'll be fine here, don't you worry a bit. Thank you again."

The visit was over, and Jill didn't want to force her hand. Mary sounded distressed, even though she made an effort to speak normally. Jill didn't wish to worry her any further. She quietly pulled the front door closed. When she got back to her Jeep and drove away into a better area she stopped and made two telephone calls.

Jill was a mandated reporter. Mary had said there were no problems. No physical bruises had been evident, but there was possible fiduciary and emotional abuse as well as neglect that she had to report by law. Yet calling in other agencies was a risk, even though it was mandated.

Jill remembered Gelsa from team B. Gelsa didn't like the way a family was treating one of her semicomatose patients, so she took him home to her own house one afternoon. That was kidnapping.

When asked why she didn't call the authorities and let them handle things, she answered, "That takes forever, and usually they don't do anything anyway." Which, generally, was true but that wasn't the point. In other ways Gelsa was a splendid nurse, and Jill hated it when she almost lost her license. Turned out the family didn't end up pressing changes after all. It seems the daughter, who was handling the care of that elderly man, liked the few days off from her caregiving duties while everything was being sorted out.

Jill knew she'd heard enough to begin her calls and see what further action should be taken.

"Michelle," she'd asked, after reaching her on the office phone line, "Are there any other options for Mary Bonsine's living arrangements? No one oversees her care. She can't keep track of her medication, and her symptoms are not good, although she underplays them."

"I'll check into that for you, Jill, any other problems there?"

"I overheard her son talking to her, and he's mean. I don't think she'd ever admit that she's worried about her situation. It's very isolated where she's living too. Especially if someone would have to make a night visit."

Michelle reassured her by saying, "I'll make some calls and get out the agency paperwork for you. See you when you get back to the office."

The second call was made to Dean Cornell, at the office. "Dean," she asked, "I need a favor. Would you get on the computer and check out this company for me, Blaston's Refrigerated Meats, Athens, Georgia?" She added the license plate number.

"I'll do what I can, Jill," Dean assured her.

"Thanks, Dean."

Jill wanted to track down anything that might help ascertain what was going on out there. Somehow, Dean had good connections on these sorts of issues. This last action was above and beyond what she was supposed to do, by law. She knew she was overstepping her boundaries there.

Jill called the Dobsons to let them know she'd be just a wee bit late. The daughter who'd answered the phone said Michelle, who'd set up the family meeting regarding care, had just called and would be along soon. Jill heard a lot of arguing or yelling in the background. That did not portend well.

Next, Jill had to respond to a strange message from a person who'd only left his name, Darrin, and a phone number. She needed to follow up on that right away, as it might be another Dobson family member.

"Hi," Darrin said when Jill called his cell phone. "Are you the one that's supposed to give me a ride from the airport to Janice's house?"

Now Jill was confused. She knew she wouldn't have promised anyone a ride in her Jeep, as it was not policy to transport any patients or their family. Car insurance coverage was very strict about that. She was trying to figure out how Darrin even got her personal cell phone number.

Not hearing an immediate answer, he added, "You know, my flight from Baltimore was delayed. Thought you might have given up on me."

The pieces fell into place. She'd lent Janice Stearn her cell phone in the emergency room. He'd had that number on his phone record and somehow wires had been crossed.

"Darrin," Jill said, "I'll tell you what. I'm right near the airport. I'll come by and get you situated on the correct airport express. I'm driving a red Jeep. Tell me, which terminal are you in?"

"The west terminal. I'll be in front of the baggage area. Thanks." Darrin said.

Jill wondered what little box she should check off on her productive day sheet. She decided since there would be no mileage factored in, and because it was on her way to the next patient, Jill would call it her break. She called Janice with the plan to get Darrin to her. Janice was pleased and apologized about the mix-up.

"No real problem," Jill stated. "I'm pleased to be of help. And, I'll see you tomorrow if you need me."

***

She was a little late getting to the Dobsons', but not too much.

Michelle was still in her pickup. She got out and greeted Jill. "I was waiting for you, because I think this little situation calls for the whistle," she said. She showed Jill a whistle on a leather strap around her neck.

"Are you kidding?" Jill asked. But then thinking of the noise and the yelling she'd heard on her earlier call, she thought it might be a good idea.

"I'll be surprised if I don't have to use it," Michelle said, as they walked up the sidewalk to the front entrance.

"Is this more of your big guns, Michelle?" Jill laughed. They were on the step and even there heard the arguing.

A man answered the door, and Jill and Michelle were escorted into a crowded living room. Mr. Dobson was lying down and most others were standing around. They showed Jill and Michelle to two chairs up against the wall. Jill remembered a previous training and how, in an environment where there may be hostility, you must have a clear escape. She smiled and moved the two chairs closer to the door.

Fortunately, even though there were many, many people crammed into the room, Jill and Michelle could identify the two daughters and two sons by their various shades of red hair, all inherited from their father. He was on the couch, looking a little weary.

Jill began, after introductions were made. "Thank you. Thank you all, so much for meeting us here."

This statement was met by a surprising quiet. After a few moments Michelle spoke.

"Yes, we're here today, and very appreciative that everyone could come on such short notice, to try and work out a plan for Bob's care. I was wondering if any of you have any ideas how to best accomplish this?"

Quiet filled the room.

Michelle tried again. "We know that, right now, the plan seems to have some holes in it. Of course we know everyone wants what's right for Mr. Dobson." She paused, then turned to Mr. Dobson and said, "Bob, do you have anything you would like to add? This meeting is for you."

Bob sighed, looked down toward the end of the couch, and gloomily looked at his feet. He then looked toward his children and said, "You know your mother would be yelling at all of you right now. I only wish she were here to see how things are. She'd still make me decide all the damned important things though." He paused a moment, then reiterated, "I wish to hell your mother was alive to see this." Then picking up speed and volume, he exclaimed, "I only know this crap has got to stop!"

Still the surprising sobering silence continued, even after that little outburst.

Then one of the daughters spoke, pointing to her sister. "This would have never happened…we wouldn't be having this problem if you picked him up on your days like you're supposed to."

That broke the ice of the accusation dam. All at once the adult children, their spouses, and even some of the older grandchildren began yelling at one another. Bob just closed his eyes and shook his head while the blame flew.

"I was late because of a flat tire."

"Today was not even my day, yet I ended up with him."

"You don't control the world."

"I can't help it if I had to work overtime."

"You always were irresponsible."

"I'm the one who always picks up his medicines."

"My wife does more than Dad's daughter, my own sister does."

"That's not fair."

And finally, "You always were Mother's favorite."

Jill sat in amazement; she wasn't afraid though. This wasn't hostility. It was a pattern, probably replayed many times. It was long-standing, sibling stuff. Regular, if unpleasant, family dynamics. She wondered if the root word *dyno*, was the same one used in dynamite. She looked at Michelle and saw that Michelle had her whistle. Even though Jill knew it was coming, Jill jumped when she heard it. It was loud and shrill. Everyone in the room stopped and looked at Michelle.

Smiling sweetly, Michelle said, "Bob, I was interested in your comment. It sounds as if you and your wife—when she was living—would at least talk about the important decisions that needed to be made. Is that right?"

"Talk or yell, they were the same things to her." Bob continued, "Anyway, she was a practical person. So after giving me hell for spoiling the kids and reviewing all my mistakes, she might say something like, well, I'm not real sure what she would say. Maybe I could think of something though. Something like, well maybe, yeah like…"

Michal Poe

One of the daughters was getting impatient with her father's long answer and was starting to interrupt. Michelle saw that and held up her hand to stop any comments as Bob was processing his thoughts. "Go on, Bob," Michelle encouraged.

"Well, Jackie is looking for a job right now. The other kids each have to lose a day's pay to take me, and maybe they could just work it out and pay Jackie for taking their day." He looked around, very pleased with his answer.

Michelle seemed pleasantly surprised by such a plausible suggestion. "That does sound like a possible solution. What do the rest of you think? One at a time, please. Jackie, especially you, does that make sense?"

Jill heard hopeful murmurs amongst the group. Jackie came over, kneeled down by the couch, and held out her arms to her dad.

He held her hands as she spoke softly. "I would love to do that, Dad."

Kate, the youngest daughter, was actually tearful. "Daddy," she asked, "Why didn't we think of that sooner?"

Bob, still pleased with himself, said very loudly again, "Just one thing though. It's damned important too. I want to stay in my own house. No more of this toting me around."

Now the noise, the pandemonium, the bedlam set in as everyone talked together, apparently hashing out the details. Interspersed were genuine sighs of relief, from the family as well as from Jill and Michelle.

Michelle passed her card around. She went to her car and came back with a prodigious amount of literature, including several wonderful pamphlets and books for some of the younger children, who were facing a death in the family for the first time. Even coloring books for the littlest ones. Jill was able to accomplish her assessment in relative peace and quiet in a corner of the living room.

Jill and Michelle left at the same time, with the permanent home address of Bob Dobson, to be added into his computer data.

"I can't believe you used that whistle."

Michelle laughed, "Wait until Ron hears. He thought he gave it to me as a joke, after that family we had last month. Remember that sports family? All the guys would settle their differences by that fake wrestling thing. I was rolled off the couch as residual damage."

Jill had to laugh too, remembering that story. "I knew I'd need it one day," Michelle said, as she got in her truck.

"Did your day get filled up?" Jill asked.

"Yes, I'm not sure I should let people know I have extra time. Now, I'm booked solid today and tomorrow." She joked as she drove off, "You guys are driving me busy."

Jill decided to run through a drive-through restaurant and get only a salad, because she had a sack lunch back at the office. She was proud of herself. She did get a salad with the light dressing, an iced tea with artificial sweetener, and only one chocolate chip cookie, even though they were on special—three for the price of two.

Jill was about halfway through her salad when she got a call from Donna. She reported that Lane would be able to see one of Jill's afternoon patients if Jill could go pronounce the reported death of Adele Fromm. Donna reported that Michelle had already called Mr. Fromm to see if any counsel would be helpful as Kim could have swung by for a quick prayer before her big funeral roast. But no, Mr. Fromm only wanted the nurse.

Jill gave her cookie a longing look. Apparently that deviation from her healthy eating plan was not meant to be. She went to the Fromms' home.

***

Just as before, Mr. Fromm met her at the door and directed her into the anteroom. Standing behind his straight-backed chair, he gave the specifics as to how he thought his wife had died. He said he was reading and sitting in the chair next to her bed when Adele started breathing in a strange manner, and she became very restless. He remembered he was told he could give her the medicine dropper with a little pain medication to help her relax. She really hadn't required it before, but he felt it was time. Before he could get the bottle top off, however, she'd stopped breathing.

"I just sat there for a while," he said, as he walked around his chair and slowly headed toward the back bedroom. "It felt so strange, Jill. Even though I knew I should be doing something, without her really there, somehow I felt…I felt paralyzed."

Mr. Fromm sighed, took a deep breath, and, stayed a step ahead of Jill, who had followed him down the hallway. Standing in the doorway he looked into the bedroom where his wife lay he said, "It was hard, I must have sat there for about twenty minutes. Just sitting with a blank mind. I finally realized I should do what she told me to do when this happened. It didn't seem like it could be real though."

"That was good thinking, Mr. Fromm," Jill commented, realizing that thought process sounded very familiar.

"Yes. I knew what she'd want. You know, straighten her up a little, and call hospice. So then I washed her face and combed her hair and called the hospice office."

"Ah, she helped you then."

"I don't suppose her voice will ever go away."

"How do you feel about that, Mr. Fromm?"

"Good. Very good," Mr. Fromm answered in his serious, shy way.

"I'm so glad," Jill said. She took a step forward but could tell that Mr. Fromm had a wide personal space boundary and wouldn't want a hug. So she only squeezed his hand in passing as she took her bag and proceeded into the bedroom. Using their bathroom, she washed her hands and gloved up. Then she carefully washed and repositioned her patient. Reverently, she checked and recorded the lack of any vital signs and filled out the details needed for the call to the coroner. She found the hospice-prescribed medicines and put them in a bag to bring out to the other room. She would explain to Mr. Fromm how he could help destroy them. She washed her hands again and made sure Adele looked as nice as possible. She turned the room light down to the dim setting. She left the room after partially closing the door to the bedroom.

Jill took her place in the original chair she'd sat in just a few days ago at that first meeting, where she'd had the crackers and milk. She called the coroner and gave a report of the expected death. He gave her the release number so she could call the mortuary. Adele was very organized and had given Jill all the information needed for these actions at their first meeting. She'd handed Jill a little filled out form entitled Helps for the Final Event. It certainly was helpful for her nurse and her husband at this time. Jill knew Adele knew how soon things would happen and how this would help smooth things for her husband. Love takes many forms, and in Adele's case that was true in the literal sense.

She let Mr. Fromm know about after-care services available. She pulled out a few grief booklets and set them on the library table, knowing Mr. Fromm might not get around to reading them, at least not yet. It seemed Adele was to have no memorial or funeral, so this was possibly the last time Jill would see him. She explained as she worked about the need for the medicine to be poured into the cat litter and sealed in the bag and then put in the trash. Mr. Fromm dutifully carried the little bag out a side door to deposit it in the trash. She heard the can lid clang shut. He didn't come back in for a while, and Jill was pretty sure she heard some crying. She finished her paperwork. Mr. Fromm eventually came back in the room. It was rather dark in there, but he didn't turn on any lights. He went down the hallway again to the bedroom door, looked in, and then came back into the main room.

"She looks good, Jill. Thanks. That's just the way she would have wanted me to do it." He went to his straight backed chair behind the library table. He seemed to be stoically looking ahead at nothing. His eyes were misty, and he was blinking a lot, but no more crying for now. He looked very lost.

After Jill finished her paperwork, wanting to stay a little longer, she took her journal out and wrote her epitaph for Adele.

Adele—Elementary Ways.
Heaven became very busy.

All the angels were being sorted as to length of wings,
Then assigned to stand in appropriately labeled circles.

After a little longer, Mr. Fromm appeared to be on automatic response. He'd called their son and his wife. They lived three hours away.

"They will stay the night and go with me to sign the final papers tomorrow morning at the funeral home," he said.

Jill knew she'd done all that Mr. Fromm would allow. Still, she didn't leave the house until after the mortuary was through taking Adele away.

Back in the car, she gave a report to her hospice office. Michelle had answered the phone and asked Jill what time she'd be back in the office. Jill told her she'd be there soon. Michelle connected her to Donna for the report. Donna said that Ron was there in the office too and wanted to ask Jill's opinion about something.

Jill listened to her other messages on the way back to the office. She only had a short time, but she could see what Ron wanted, turn in her current paperwork, and get the information she needed to save a trip later.

***

When she arrived back at the office, Ron was in the bathroom, so his question would have to wait. Meanwhile she and Michelle went over their problem cases. Michelle said she thought she'd call the Fromms' son tomorrow morning and let him know how hospice bereavement services could help him and his father. She would see if he would allow a visit, since she would not be a stranger. Michelle felt someone would be needed to check up on Mr. Fromm from time to time, and this would give her an in—or not. Anyway she'd try.

Michal Poe

Michelle really needed to talk about that other patient, Mary Bonsine.

Over the past year, Jill and Michelle had slowly discovered that Dean had some serious contact sources he divulged to no one. This had come to be very useful from time to time. So far they hadn't abused this discovery. It came in handy in this case because Michelle said Dean had just told her that there was no such company as the one Jill had asked him to look up. Dean had also found a way to get information about the truck. The truck's license appeared to be a current one, but not for a refrigerated truck.

Michelle had called the elder abuse agency to see if there was any kind of record on Mary Bonsine and to run the case by them. She'd told them she was calling because Mary might not have access to her medications and was mixing up those she did have. The agency social worker was very familiar with this lady. She verified that it was hard to keep a handle on Mrs. Bonsine, because she moved every three to four months. The county abuse agency was always getting vague calls about her. Never anything real specific, they said. At one time, an investigation revealed that all signs pointed to the son running a chop shop, but by the time the investigator got there, the place was emptied out.

"See," Jill said. "None of that surprises me. Will they investigate now?"

"Yes, but they can't triage it as a high priority. There was one investigator, a man who worked in the department who went out the last time there was a report, and he said he'd be only too happy to get the chance to chase this case down. The earliest he or anybody could go is tomorrow morning."

"These kinds of cases are so hard," Jill responded to Michelle's report. "I couldn't tell for sure if Mary was scared of her son, or maybe she truly thinks he needs her, or she doesn't want to go against her husband's wishes or…well, I don't know what other complications we don't even know about."

"We have no option but to look into these things," Michelle commiserated with Jill's uneasiness in reporting. "Oh, the screener at the county warned that the trick is to not tip off anyone in case there is something illegal going on, as they suspect there is.'"

"I don't think anything I said would have done that."

"Good," Michelle said, "I'll bet you if they asked Mary, she'd say she was fine right where she is. If there's no physical, emotional, or fiduciary abuse that can be verified, there's nothing anyone can do. It's a free country. It's her decision to make questionable choices."

"I know," Jill said. "That's good. But it's still hard to watch."

"I've been going over her record from when she was hospitalized a few months ago. I saw a lot of information about the daughter who visited her there. The nursing report gave that daughter as the main contact. But then the mother, our patient, decided to go back to live with the son. My job is to see if staying with that daughter or another living arrangement is even feasible for her. When the county abuse guy calls me tomorrow, he'll want to know."

"I feel better with you taking the lead on this Michelle. Thank you so much."

"By the way," Michelle added, "Dano called me and said the bartender said I'd left some shoes behind the bar. The guy was gonna throw them away, but Dano rescued them. I told him they were yours. Can you pick them up tonight after work?"

"All alone, in a bar?" Jill questioned.

"Jill! It's done all the time. Sometimes I can't believe you're only ten years older than me."

Jill defended herself. "Well it's another generation."

Michelle went on, "Around five or six is a good time. Everybody's getting happy, nobody's drunk."

"I need those shoes; they were my best work pair. Don't be surprised if I call you falling off the bar stool, loaded," Jill teased.

"That's the most ridiculously impossible thing I've heard all day."

Jill knew that was true. She liked having fun, but it didn't involve any substances, except, of course, prodigious amounts of tea, hot or cold.

"Do you need a hug or something?" Michelle asked. "Looks like these cases took a lot out of you today."

"No, it's just Thursday."

"I see." She knew.

Ron was finished in the bathroom and came into the workroom acting a little shy. He was dressed in a suit. It was a nice color for him, but it didn't fit very well. "What do you think?" he asked Jill and Michelle.

"You mean after it's tailored?" Michelle asked.

"I like the color," Jill said.

"So you think it's too big? That's what the guy said but he wanted me to go a size smaller, and those weren't on sale. This is the first suit I've bought, even been in, since my wedding."

"We'll need Dean's advice on this," Michelle said as she went to his office to get him.

Ron looked to Jill. "That Wedge thing is turning into something more than I expected. Not only am I going to attend, but they want me to speak. Bill said I have to wear a suit if I'm representing hospice."

"How did Bill get this involved?" Jill queried.

"Mrs. Wedge called and wants to give me all the rest of this season's tickets and upgrade it to an even better, private sky box. Bill's thinking about it, wondering how that will fall out. Needed a suit anyway."

Dean came out of his office and went straight to Ron, letting him know how he'd want the tailor to make the adjustments. Ron looked so uncomfortable even talking about it that Dean agreed to meet Ron after work at the store where he'd purchased the suit.

***

During the drive to the Darterville Mortuary and Cemetery for the roast, Jill flipped off the speakerphone attached to her sun visor. She needed a few minutes to think about her after work task. She'd never in her life been in a bar alone. She must be so out of it. Strong as Jill was, it did sound daring. She saw nothing really wrong about it, she had a perfect right to go into a bar in broad daylight, but she admitted to herself that unless she'd had this errand there was no way she'd do such a thing. *I guess I've never had reason*, she thought. *I've never gone looking for men, didn't like to drink, usually ran errands with a son or a mother in tow...And,* that was about it. It would be a first. What the heck, she really needed those shoes. Her thoughts even scared her—they were so ancient, so pre-feminist. You'd think she was eighty years old, and even that thought was unfair to octogenarians.

    The directions Kim had left at the office for those who could make it to the funeral led Jill to the rear entrance of the graveyard. Jill had never been around to that side before. But she noted it was nice and shady and there was a small, square stone building behind the several tables that were being set up on a level grassy area. A very large banner draped the little building, almost entirely covering its front, proclaiming: WELCOME TO SHANE'S ROAST! Kim was already there, and she and an older man were helping with the tables. Two other ladies and the widow were draping the dais table, which was directly in front of the banner. Jill helped them find the tablecloths and put small floral arrangements on each table. It was really turning out to be a warm and cozy little area. If it weren't for the headstones lining one side it would be a lovely place for a wedding.

    When the caterers arrived, Jill knew she was in for a treat. The Greatest Ever Food Service Co. set up more tables along one side. Everything looked so delicious. There were hors d'oeuvres, a table with cold salads, one with hot foods, a large choice of artisan breads, and several lovely looking glass-covered dessert plates. The table settings were beautiful gold-rimmed china and cloth napkins. My, my…between that wonderful breakfast made by Stan's wife and now this spread, Jill knew she'd have to forego dinner. She was grateful she hadn't had time to eat the cookie and the rest of her lunch after all.

    A beverage table was being set up, and Mrs. Shane poured a glass of tea for herself, motioning Jill over. They hugged and she thanked Jill for coming. She asked Jill if she could greet people as they came, get them set up at a table, and let them know that they could start eating.

Then, Mrs. Shane left with one of the funeral home men, saying she had a few more details to finalize.

People were arriving in groups of two or three. As Jill greeted them, she recognized a few of the comedians. Most were really up in age. Two were heading off to the side to have a smoke, and Jill overheard one of the funeral workers inform them that they needed to pull a couple of chairs over if they needed to sit because the headstones were off limits.

"Even the one that almost looks like a nice bench?" asked one of the comedians, apparently quite serious.

"Yes, it's all off limits," the man repeated.

Jill had been expecting a good comeback line. She heard none. Maybe it was true what was said of comedians that in real life, when not on the stage, they were very serious people.

Kim continued to go over her notes, with a worried furrow in her forehead. Jill played hostess until she was interrupted by a phone message. The return number was Michelle's with 911 after it. This was an agreed-upon code for "urgent."

Fortunately and surprisingly, Donna showed up about that time. Jill was able to have her take over the role as greeter. Now Jill could go and answer that call without worrying Mrs. Shane.

Walking back toward the funeral home's main building, Jill realized how pleased she was that Donna could come. She imagined Donna would head home after the memorial. Jill hoped so, after that scare this morning. Jill was sure Donna and that panel could give their hospice another chance to show a better face to the community. Donna hadn't asked her to be on the panel. Jill had heard from Michelle that Lane would appear as the representative nurse on the panel. Jill wondered why Donna would choose such a new nurse. Although Jill was very glad she wouldn't have another after work time assignment for Friday night, she'd realized she'd been a little miffed because she wasn't chosen.

 Jill went back into the vestibule and found a good place to sit in a far corner, so as not to disturb anyone who would enter. It was cushy, comfortable, quiet, and so nicely decorated. She loved the low, soft chairs and glass dishes of hard candy set out here and there. She began to make her urgent and other phone calls.

 Michelle was very excited to tell Jill how things were turning out with the Bonsine case. It appeared the elder abuse guy had called the sheriff, not the city police, since that industrial area was outside the city limits. Michelle said there'd been an ongoing investigation into this son. Now a plan was put in order for an early-morning raid on the place as they suspected it was full of stolen vehicles. The sheriff was very glad to hear, Michelle reported, that there was an agency involved so they wouldn't have to take the elderly parents into custody. They wanted Michelle to meet them as soon as she got their call, and then to help the county elder abuse man coordinate the arrangements for the hospice patient they knew lived on the grounds. They were thinking it would be good to have a nurse there too, to oversee any health need. They said they could transport the patient to the hospital if that was needed. Michelle wanted to make sure Jill had her cell phone turned on, as she'd given the sheriff, Jill's contacts as well.

Michelle was young and had a lot of energy for this kind of situation. It was more a social worker's issue. Jill had been around long enough to know to expect some anguish. The situation had to be handled for the safety of Mary and her even more elderly, and probably just as frail, spouse. It was out of their hands now. Michelle also said she was leaving Donna the message that Bill had already talked to the authorities and okayed Jill and Michelle's roles. Jill thanked Michelle and assured her she'd be available early Friday morning. Jill needed to go back to the roast and get a glass of iced tea for herself, but first she had to make a few more calls.

The next call was to Bennett. Apparently he'd tried to get ahold of her Wednesday night and was going to let her know he really needed to talk to her, but he'd found out she'd been out dancing. On the message left Wednesday evening, he'd sounded very sweet, saying; "Jill I thought I was your dancing partner." First hot, then cold from Bennett. She had no idea what his true feelings were and had even less insight about her true feelings for him. This dating thing took a lot of stamina. It must be a sport meant for the young. She called his private, special back number.

His hygienist took the call.

Jill explained Bennett wanted to get ahold of her.

"I'll check," the hygienist said.

Jill waited a minute or so, wondering if calling the back line was the right thing to do.

"He asked me to tell you he's in the middle of a procedure. He wants to know if you will remain available so he could call you in a few minutes."

"Sure," Jill answered.

Michal Poe

She called home but remembered Jason would be at his afternoon job. She didn't even know for sure, where he was working. She left a message on his cell phone, asking him to pick up something for himself and Stina for dinner, as Jill would be stuffed by the time she got home. She also asked for a little time with him to discuss the idea of hiring extra help on weekends.

The day care home rarely took clients on the weekends anymore. Not even on Sundays. Fern said she had to put that in place to keep her own sanity. Jill could understand that. But Jill's mom was about to the point where constant supervision was necessary. Jill had put all the safety tips into practice. Stina had a bracelet with information—her condition, her address, and medications—on it. Jill had read an article that proposed the idea, in all seriousness, of embedding a computer chip somewhere on the confused person's body. After all, jewelry such as bracelets could be removed or accidentally broken. It made sense on paper. It certainly seemed, on first thought, so ideal. They did this on pets, and a pet would have a better chance of finding its way home than her demented mother. Second thoughts immediately came to mind, and then it seemed so invasive, so "mark of the beast" like.

Jill had made sure her property was safely fenced. All the doors had high locks where her mom couldn't reach them if she got confused in the middle of the night. The knobs on the oven, stove, and heater were removed. The medicine cabinet was locked. Cleaning materials and solvents were on a high shelf in the garage area. The water heater temperature had been lowered. Jill was doing everything humanly possible, but she knew there was no way to totally control the environment. Her mom hadn't taken any falls yet, and Stina didn't wander around the house at night. She was still sleeping well. These things were a blessing.

Her work messages included some that had been forwarded to her. She started to listen but realized she'd have to sort them out tomorrow after team. She was interested in the first one. It was Janice Stearn thanking her for getting Darrin to her safely and letting her know that they were catching up on twenty years of love. That sounded pretty interesting. Knowing she needed to be off the phone soon, she made a short return phone call to Janice. She was happy to hear Janice didn't sound so out of breath. She heard someone singing in the background. Jill asked about that.

Janice said, "Didn't Darrin tell you? He's an entertainer. Doesn't he have a wonderful voice?"

Jill agreed. She congratulated Janice on her good fortune to have such a special man waiting in the wings for her. She made an appointment to see Janice the early part of next week.

Then Bennett's call came through. He, too, had a wonderful voice. It was the first thing that had attracted Jill to him. It was still comforting. But this conversation was just more of the same—the continued ambivalence. She could detect that he wanted her to make some decisions for him, even about his own sexuality. His concerns about being bisexual came up and haunted him. Anyone could tell how torn he felt. Jill didn't understand. After all this was the twenty-first century.

"Oh Jill," he said in his lovely manner, "You know I'm still wanting a traditional relationship."

"I see," Jill said.

Michal Poe

"But I can't really seem to commit to anything. I just want to be content, to feel whole."

Jill didn't want or need a commitment. However, it seemed Bennett thought a commitment to a woman would change things for him, make him happy. Jill couldn't be responsible for making anybody happy. She'd learned that lesson the hard way. Even with her son, her mother, her friends, and her patients, she'd finally figured out that wasn't her role. In her marriage, that caregiving bent of hers didn't work out at all. She certainly wouldn't force any decisions for Bennett. She didn't want to be his "swing vote"—the person who would tip things for him, change him somehow. It had to come from him.

Jill began to pace around the reception room as she continued to talk to Bennett.

After more conversation, they realized they were just rehashing what they always talked about. So although both she and Bennett sounded sad, right there on the phone they agreed to take a small hiatus. Then they'd try to reconvene as friends. From there they would see where it led. Jill was hoping they could retain a friendship. He was a wonderful man. Her heart felt tender, and the words were spoken haltingly and lovingly.

"It may work out, it may not," Jill said, "but, Bennett, I think you're a good man. Please, remember, I want to keep in touch."

On her walk back to the funeral, Jill felt somehow free, and also very tired.

Hook ups! Must be a young person's game. Oh, how she longed for an instant relationship as, say, the McCarthys', nudist camp and all. Sixty years together and still interesting to one another, even when totally undressed. Or like Randy and Roger, who found such comfort and strength together in dire times. Heck, she'd even settle for Joyce Sealy and her husband's relationship, minus the heaps of junk. Romantic love everywhere, except for Jill. So as not to continue to feel sorry for herself, she headed back to the food.

Jill had been gone long enough to know she might have missed some fun. She heard the laughter and the talking before she rounded the corner on her way back to the grassy area. The funeral-memorial-roast was in full swing. Mrs. Shane, a few comedians, and Chaplain Kim were sitting behind the dais. Behind them off to the left was a closed gray coffin. They must have moved that in when Jill was off on her phone calls. The chair at the table beside Mrs. Shane was empty, and on the table in front of it was a nice framed picture of Shane in his younger years. Two older women and the wait personnel were circulating around the tables on the grassy square, refilling plates and glasses.

Jill spied Donna at a small table with three or four others. She slipped in next to her, since there was an empty chair right beside Donna. Almost immediately, Jill had an iced tea and a plateful of food set before her by a server. With one ear she listened to some of the talk around the table and with the other to the current comedian on the agenda. Kim must have already introduced him some time ago, because Jill had heard his voice amplified through a microphone all the way on her way back to rejoin the group.

The elderly comedian was standing with the help of a cane. He said, "Yes, Shane told me, 'My father came to this country and made a name for himself. The name he chose was…Shane.'"

Michal Poe

There was a little scattered laughter as he continued. "His dad always told him, 'Shane, listen to your conscience.' But Shane said, 'Nah, mom always said don't talk to strangers!'" This got a little bigger laugh.

The comedian saw that a few people had gotten up from their table for some reason, and he yelled out, "Folks, where ya going? The roast isn't over. You'll be here permanently soon enough. Seriously, I guess you know that Penton is up next. Who could blame you for leaving?" That got him a few more laughs before he sat down.

Kim introduced Mr. Penton, saying she'd heard he was a longtime friend of Shane, who had a bet with him as to which one would go first.

Another man in a mustard-colored suit quickly stood up.

He bellowed, "Yeah, that slob Shane won. This ain't no dress rehearsal!" He twirled his lime green tie around.

Penton, now standing, said, "Unlock your knees, Strickner, and sit down." Penton continued. "Shane was always a lazy bastard, and now he gets to rest while I have to continue to look at your ugly mugs! Har, Har, Har. Well seriously, folks, we are here to honor Shane. He wanted to be a comedian in the worst way…and he succeeded. He bombed so many times, he thought he was in the Mideast. Har, har, har. But hey, he was sharp. Last time I saw Shane I was kidding him, I said, 'My memory isn't what it used to be. Mind telling me your name again?' Shane says, 'How soon do you need to know?' Har, har, har."

Other people at the tables were starting to circulate amongst themselves as this current comedian continued with more of the same. Jill noted that she knew the names of many of the people at the various tables, who'd apparently arrived while she'd been on the phone. Jill knew Shane was in show business a long time, and she was glad so many had come to honor him. She thought Mrs. Shane must be pleased.

Penton kept going on and on, mostly old jokes, but he was trying.

One man at the table next to Jill was taking a call. His hearing aide was obvious. He was talking loudly. Other people were so distracted that no one seemed to care.

"That agent doesn't know crap. I could do a better job than her!" the man yelled into his cell phone.

"Hey, pipe down back there," Penton said from the dais. "You has-been. We're here to honor one of the greatest has-beens ever. Har, har, har." Mr. Penton motioned toward the picture of Shane on the table. "Look at him. He was so thin he had to wear a life jacket in the tub to keep from going down the drain! Har, har, har. His wife's a good cook though. I didn't understand how he stayed so skinny. Shane said to me, 'Penton, I'm dyspeptic.' I said in this business it's like that military thing they had, 'don't ask, don't tell.' Har, har, har."

Even though he was losing his audience, Mr. Penton continued, but this time on a little more sober note. "Whatever joke I could tell, though, Shane could tell two that were better. He was ahead of the curve. Hell, since he could never draw or walk a straight line, he drew the curve."

Then Penton, seemingly not comfortable with his slightly more serious quips, quickly reverted to some well-worn one-liners. Jill imagined this guy could go on forever. She saw Kim wriggling in her seat and knew that signal. Sure enough, right then, during a slight pause while Penton was laughing at yet another of his own tired jokes, Kim jumped up and took Mrs. Shane's elbow. She helped her up to the center podium. She hastily thanked Mr. Penton. The comedian's face looked miffed to have been cut off, but he did sit down.

While this was happening, Donna got a tap on the shoulder. An older man from an adjacent table had leaned way over toward her. Both Jill and Donna recognized him as a big-name comic, still working.

"Are you Shane's daughter?" he asked.

"No," Donna said, "I didn't know he had a daughter."

"He might not have one, but it's always funny when a long-lost daughter shows up at the funeral. Don't you think so?"

Donna looked at the man rather open-mouthed. Jill had never seen Donna so tongue-tied. Donna cast a helpless look toward Jill. Jill didn't know what to say either, so she just smiled calmly and continued to enjoy her crème brulée.

From the podium, Kim continued, "Thank you so much. I know Shane would be delighted to know how all of you've held forth at his roast. Now, Mrs. Shane, our own Esther, wants to say a few words."

Things became a little quieter. "Thank you for being here," Esther began. "You know, Shane kept me young. Seems like he never got too old to learn some new way to be foolish." Esther Shane was smiling, but people didn't seem to know if that was meant to be a joke or not.

She continued in a slower, heartfelt manner. "Our lives were busy. Shane traveled so much. When it was hard, I'd just think, how could I not love a man whose only goal in life was to make people laugh? I hardly ever get a word in edgewise with him. I loved that man, still do, and always will. But it seems I haven't stopped talking since he died. I've started telling the same hackneyed jokes. Well, not all his jokes were bad, but they're the ones I remembered, as I see many of you remembered as well." Esther smiled again and then tearing up she added, "I guess he'll always live on. Such a good man, such a love, shy in some ways…really."

Things were quiet now. A few in the audience were dabbing at genuine tears. Behind the dais there was a little activity as two of the funeral men had arrived.

She spoke again, but in an upbeat tempo. "But, we're not here for me. We're here for the roast. So let's get on with Shane's last wish."

The casket was in position to the left of the cement building. Part of the banner had been loosened on the extreme left side. Now the gathered group could see, in small bronze letters, the word *Crematorium*. The door was opened; the funeral men rolled the casket in partway, and then slightly tilted it. The coffin slid off the wheeled cart, right onto the shelf inside. The men wheeled the cart out, and Kim joined Mrs. Shane outside the door but fairly near the casket. Mrs. Shane blew a kiss toward the coffin and pushed the button to close the door. As it closed, Kim began a prayer. Everyone was sitting glued to his or her chairs. Not a corny word was heard.

"Into Your hands we commend this soul," Kim intoned. "Oh Lord, may he find eternal rest in Your love."

The same comedian sitting near Janet was now open-mouthed himself. "Wow," he said. "This real roast is even better than an illegitimate child! That Shane…wow!"

Michal Poe

People were quiet and then slowly pushed back their chairs and formed a line to pass by the widow and give hugs and brief words of support.

Kim, Donna, and Jill were grouped together nearby. Kim quietly explained to Jill and Donna that she'd discussed the crematorium issue with Dean before she'd suggested it as a possibility to Esther. He'd explained to her that following the families wishes right before and after the death was very important for long term healing of the grief reaction. Since Esther definitely wanted to be present when Darterville funeral home did the cremation, they'd talked to the funeral director and he'd seen no problem having as many friends and family there as Esther wished. Kim said Mr. Darter told her that their next ad campaign, soon to be sent out across the city, had their new motto, *Darterville Funeral Home—We're Here for the Living!*

As many funerals as she'd attended, though, Jill had never actually seen such a thing before. She was ashamed that all she could think of when it was happening is that it looked as if a giant pizza was being slid off the big wooden paddle into the oven.

Donna, Kim, and Jill were able to leave the graveside affair together, after giving their business cards and their own condolences to Esther. Donna took a minute before she went home to let Jill know that she'd asked Lane to be on the panel because the other hospices wanted balance. None of them had a nurse under age forty. Most were much older. The consortium thought it would look bad. Even though Donna and all the nurses knew the nursing shortage was real, and retirement for many loomed large, they wanted to show hospice as an option for even young nurses. Jill understood completely. She had been the youngest nurse herself in hospice when she'd first begun. In a way, it seemed like such a lonely job, driving around all day. But for Jill it didn't feel that way now. She felt so connected with most of her co-workers.

Jill helped Kim get what was needed back into her old white station wagon. It was still stuffed with various items Kim needed daily. Since the nurses had complained to Kim that their supplies were being squeezed out by her stuff, Kim had begun to use her backseat for her books. There were books on funeral rituals, religions of the world, and prayers for the living, dying, and the in-between. *Prayers and Homilies for the Deceased of all the Ages, Through the Ages* was printed in English and Spanish. Kim was bilingual. One intriguing book Jill had looked through was *How Culture Affects the Perception of the Afterlife*. It had many woodcut illustrations, being the equivalent of a coffee table book for hospice workers.

Since Jill didn't have to get back to the office, she and Kim had some time to talk. Kim showed her the envelopes she'd received. Jill hadn't noticed, but on the dais table were several envelopes entitled, "In Lieu of Flowers." Underneath were a few charities that Shane wanted to support. Community Hospice was identified on that list. Several guests had put an X in that spot, and Kim was pleased as this was the first time she'd had a chance to use this more formal way of solicitation.

"I'm not sure asking right out like that is seemly." Jill commented.

"Oh, yes," Kim said. "Some funeral homes had the envelopes premade, as a courtesy. That way at the time the family came in to sign the final papers, the list could be offered and imprinted with the chosen charities."

It was accomplished at the same time the funeral leaflets were printed. Kim thought it a good idea, because although people may want to give something to a scholarship fund or some other cause, unless they had the envelope with the address of where to send it later if they wanted, it was never done. The way Kim explained it, it seemed reasonable, and Jill was a reasonable person. Jill saw that the funeral home website address was on there and contributions could be made via the Internet. At least she didn't see the Facebook connection.

"After today," Jill stated, "I have no idea of what could possibly be next."

"Me either," Kim said. "It's an exciting time we live in, though. Lots of changes everywhere."

"That sums you up, Kim. You find change exciting; most of us find it painful."

***

Jill thought about that painful aspect on her way home, as she did have that one stop to make. She hoped no one would see her car in the bar's parking lot.

Jill remembered one nurse Jill was very happy to see fired several years ago. He'd been caught drinking on the job, twice. The first time he'd talked his way out of it. Reaction to a cough medicine or some such thing, he'd said. But he was permanently locked out of the hospice office after a bartender called the hospice manager and asked, "Who is this strange guy that stops by for a drink every afternoon and brags about carrying needles and shit with him in his car?" Jill couldn't remember exactly what happened to him or if the company brought charges against him.

It was not work hours, she reminded herself. Nevertheless, she sat in the parking lot at Dano's for a while, until it sunk in that that was not the reason for her hesitation. There were only three other cars there. She started to get out and then decided not to. This is insane, she thought. What was her problem? She got out, slammed her door a little too hard, and strode into the club. Going straight to the bar, she was surprised to find Dano there. He was arranging glasses.

"Hello, Cinderella," he said.

"Hello, Prince Charming," she retorted.

"I have your shoes; I'll get them in a minute. Want anything to drink? Can you stay for ten minutes at least?"

"Are my shoes the ransom?"

Dano looked as if he just had to smile. He appeared very pleased with Jill's ability to banter. Jill saw that he certainly was flirting.

"It's the Sicilian in me," Dano joked. "Wants to play every advantage."

"I'm flattered. Remember, though, it's the shoes that'll get you ten minutes of my time."

"Fair enough. How about something to drink?"

"It's late in the day, but I have a ways to drive, so how about a diet cola."

"Living dangerously? Oh I guess you know, you only live once." He laughed this time.

Jill noticed he looked entirely different when he smiled or laughed.

Dano was a swift bartender. The cola was set before her in a jiffy, along with a new small bowl of salted nuts.

"How long have you been doing your job?" Dano asked.

Michal Poe

"Today, only nine hours. But total, I've been in nursing almost twenty years." Jill answered, as she took a sip of her soda.

"Aren't you worried about burn-out? Don't you get tired of dealing with people all day?" Dano continued with his questions.

"If I wasn't such a good listener, I wouldn't have caught that this was your own personal sentiment coming through. How long have you been in your business?"

Dano looked at her. She could see his mind working. Seeing that maybe it was his own thoughts that had come through. Seeing that he was surprised at the truth of what she'd said, and also pleased she'd illuminated the thoughts he must have been having of late.

"You're dangerous," he said.

"This coming from a professed Sicilian?"

Dano laughed, "Hey, I'm proud of my heritage," he answered, obviously glad to get on another subject.

"Me too," Jill said.

"What is your ethnicity? If I may ask. I've been trying to figure that out since I met you a few days ago. I was thinking, could it be Indian, Mexican, or Sicilian even? I couldn't get it. Couldn't place your beauty, your striking look, in any category."

Jill put her cola down. Jill hadn't missed his compliment but went right to the question. "You were right on a few counts. I'm multi-ethnic. I call it ME. My father was French, Black, and English, that we know of. My mother is Navajo, Mexican, Italian, and German, for sure. Probably other things in there too. Oh, and for the record, Lurline is of Welsh heritage. Since I noticed your interest in her as well."

"I like to cover all bases," Dano admitted. "You didn't look very available."

"No comment," Jill smiled.

"Hey, let me show you around my club," Dano said, "I've done a lot since I bought the place."

Jill took another drink of her cola before she set her drink down. "I saw most of the place the other night, but I already have one suggestion for you."

"What's that, the poles again?" Dano asked as he came around to the front of the bar.

Jill was pleased he'd remembered her comment. "No, it's the women's bathroom. It could use some updates."

"You should see the men's! But yes, I knew that. One of my ex-wives said she'd do it if I kept up the alimony."

"Child support?" Jill asked.

She knew it was none of her business but concluded it was the darkness in the place that brought out things she wouldn't have said in the light. She guessed she was also celebrating the fact that she and Bennett had made a decision and she felt free to flirt.

"Two grown daughters," Dano responded to her last question. "And you, how about you?"

"Only one ex. Thank God. He's never been much in the picture. A wonderful son about to choose a college, and my mother. I take care of her."

"Me too!" Dano said, sounding surprised and very pleased to hear it. "I take care of my mother too. She lives with me, kind of an elder home thing, right on the property. I don't dare call it a Granny flat. It's part of my heritage too. I'm the oldest son. She's something else though. Oh and my two daughters, they're half sisters. They live out of state right now."

Dano talked during the entire time he led Jill around pointing out improvements he'd made here and there. He stopped in front of one of the poles. "I asked the building guy, when I changed out the place, 'What about the stripper poles?' The guy said I'd have to make a new use of them because they are supports for the roof! I haven't thought of any uses though."

"Hmm," Jill pondered.

"Maybe they could be posts for tying horses," Dano said.

"I know. Build models of different kinds of working horses around each pole, and throw on saddles. It'd be a more comfortable seat for the real cowboys. Or do it like a carousel and charge for the ride. Oh, and one more thing, Dano."

"Yes?" Dano responded.

"My shoes. I really do need to get home."

"Okay, a deal's a deal, and my ten minutes are up. Truth be told, I've been pleased to get even that much time. I've accomplished a lot in my life with only ten-minute slots."

Jill couldn't think of a credible comeback comment, so she just smiled again.

He headed over to the bar, retrieved her shoes, and brought them to her. "What are you going home to tonight?" he asked.

"Voles," Jill answered. "They're taking over the place. I have to think of a good way to get rid of them without having to resort to using poison."

"I have a dog that hates vermin. You tell me when, and I'll bring him over."

"I may do that Dano, thanks," Jill said as she walked toward the door.

"I'm serious," Dano added, in a rather low, intense tone, as if he didn't want the few other patrons whom he'd ignored during the ten minutes to overhear him.

Jill turned and looked at him. He was a good-looking guy. She liked him, although he wasn't quite her type. He was fairly tall, muscular, and probably near her age. He had the good thing with his mother going for him though. And she remembered, in fact she'd caught again, the faint scent of a cigar. She knew the olfactory nerves went directly to the brain. No filters were in operation. The frontal lobes were totally left out. Now that could be dangerous.

"I'll think about it," she said in the same low, intense manner. "Bye for now."

Dano opened the club's door for her and would have followed her out to her car if she hadn't hurried.

Jill had to admit, on her drive home, that it was kind of fun exchanging quips with a good-looking, grown man. She was liking this new game plan. She'd put no more real effort at discovery. Especially no more blind dates. She'd just allow things to happen slowly. Being able to banter in the dark bar made her remember when Jason was little and they would sit on the porch in the dark and talk. It was conducive to deeper conversation. That had to be it; the brighter the light, the more cautious the talk. She bet that nobody got to know anyone on the beach in broad daylight. That is, nothing about the inner self, she amended. Probably all, maybe more than they needed to know about the outer. But still, any new relationship would take up a lot of her time. She'd been torn even about taking the ten minutes tonight because she wanted to have time with Jason to talk about schools and his job.

***

When she got home, she was met by Jason, who told her that he'd already put Stina to bed after she had a nutrition drink because she seemed very tired when he'd picked her up.

Jill called Fern, who said she'd noticed a difference in Stina and wondered if she was coming down with something or just moving on down a notch in her function. Jill thanked her for the information.

She went to check on her mom after thanking Jason for getting her off to bed. Stina looked comfortable. She was sleeping soundly and breathing normally. Jill felt her forehead, noting there was probably no fever. Jill would check again in the morning. She might have to take her to the doctor tomorrow though. She would certainly have to call during the day and see if Fern thought Stina was still acting a little under the weather. Any of Stina's medicines could be causing some kind of reaction. Jill kept her hand on Stina's forehead a little longer. She thought of all the times her mom had helped her when she was ill. There was nothing more comforting to her than to have her mom's cool hand on her forehead. She carefully leaned down and gave her mom a light kiss. Stina was becoming more demented and was not as affectionate as she had been. Jill knew that it was because Stina was becoming progressively less familiar with her surroundings. Jill had been informed that Stina would find it harder to recognize the people in her life, and that would make her retreat further inside herself, where it was safer. Jill had to steal the little kisses she gave her mom. You could read or talk about these things at a dementia group, but until it happened, she realized there wasn't much she could have done to prepare herself. It was distressing.

She found Jason sitting at the kitchen counter eating toast. Jill heated up some leftovers for dinner, and while they ate they had time to talk. He said his job was at the Burger Barn Place. The franchise was fairly close by. He said they liked his work and he'd already been told by the manager that instead of a server he could train as a fry cook if he wanted to work on weekends.

He laughed when he said that. "Mom, you know I can't cook. Think of the training!"

"Are you really considering doing that?" Jill asked.

"Nope, I'm not. Hope you're not disappointed. Hey, you know Sherrice taught me a better way to make peanut butter and jelly sandwiches. I made some for lunch tomorrow. She mixes the stuff together before she puts it on the bread so it doesn't slip around when you bite into it."

"Ever upward and onward son," Jill joked. "Did you make one for me?"

"Yeah, and I left an apple for you too."

Jill leaned over and gave her son a kiss on his cheek. She didn't have to steal it, and he gave her a tight hug in return.

She grabbed her sandwich and apple off the counter and put them in a lunch bag for tomorrow. Then she changed her clothes and went out to her fields to count the new vole trails. She looked toward the neighboring home farther down the rural road. All was quiet there. She missed her old neighbors, but that family had moved out about a month ago. No watering was done on their land anymore, and Jill concluded that was probably why her vole population had suddenly increased. Jill wanted everything to be organic, so she wasn't about to put down anything toxic. She needed to call the agricultural extension and ask about alternative methods. She'd put it on her to do list. She had to do something quickly before her kitchen garden was attacked. She'd already put up fencing to keep out rabbits and deer, but she hadn't thought about burrowing pests. She was especially worried that all her lavender fields would be eaten up.

She took a short run in the waning light. It was slightly cool out, and she was again grateful that she'd been able to take up running. After her shower and feeling very refreshed, she checked on her mother one more time. Stina looked peaceful. Her light snoring was a sign she was resting well. Jill went back in the kitchen and asked Jason not to stay up too late studying.

Jill headed for her bedroom. She liked how she had redecorated it. She'd found some period furniture and a four-poster bed that was high off the floor. It had a little stepstool beside it, but Jill liked to jump up onto her bed. She felt like it was an island in a lagoon. When she'd first put the bed up, she actually had slipped out of it a few times getting up in the middle of the night. Off and on over her lifetime, her mom had made beautiful wool rugs that turned out to be a good landing material. She was about ready to make the jump when Jason gave a knock at her door.

He peeked his head in. "Mom, I forgot to ask, is it alright if Sherrice's dad takes me to look at trading in the Chevy sometime this weekend? You can go, too, but I know you don't know a lot about cars, and Rob said he was once a used-car salesman. So I could probably get the best deal with him along."

Jill sighed, she hoped not too loudly. "Yes, Jason you do what you feel is best. But remember, I have the pink slip, so call me before you actually think seriously about any deals, okay?"

"Yep, Rob already told me, no signing the first time in. He said the deals only get better and better. As the stakes go up, the price comes down."

"Good advice, son. Goodnight, I love you."

"'Night, mom, love you too."

Even if the words were sometimes perfunctory, Jill loved the sound of that phrase.

FRIDAY

The next morning, Jill awakened in the early dawn. She'd heard banging and the faint beep-beep of a truck backing up. The carried sound of an excited dog barking was new too. Looking out her upstairs room, she could see down the road that a new neighbor must be moving in. That was a quick turnaround on the sale. She was glad she'd have a fairly close neighbor again.

Jill ate her breakfast and put on some farm work clothes. Her mom was still sleeping soundly. She seemed to be doing fine—still no fever, but Jill thought she was breathing a little heavy.

Jill knew her mom couldn't get up and down the stairs for too much longer, so she was going to section off the dining room, which was seldom used. She was planning on making a little sitting room with a day bed for her mom. It was close to the downstairs bathroom and would work perfectly. She'd been slowly introducing the idea to her mother. Stina was getting more and more averse to any kind of change in her routine. Someone usually had to be with her when she moved around. They'd have to position her just right and give a little support. This weekend, she and Jason would finish up the house to make it more comfortable for her mother. That was her task. A task to be accomplished with love and laughter, she'd decided.

Michal Poe

Her brother, C.J., and her nieces were coming for a visit in a few weeks, and she wanted to show them how nice things were for Stina. He'd suggested more than once that maybe it was time to find a real nursing home for their mother. He reminded her there were some of Stina's savings to use for it and then the state aid would have to take over. Jill simply couldn't do that unless her mother truly became impossible to care for in a home setting. She needed to talk to her brother about hiring care for weekends. She wanted to get his approval. C.J. would always be her big brother. She wanted him to approve of her actions. Jill was willing to use her own money for the weekend help, to make her mom's day care money last longer. C.J. helped his mom by buying things for her, things Stina mostly couldn't use now. So Jill was glad he could come to see the situation first hand. He would be shocked, even though it had only been six months since he'd seen her. Their mom's dementia had progressed more quickly than either of them expected. She wanted to put his mind at ease. Jill knew it would make him sad to see his mom's world was getting so small. Jill only hoped Stina's world wasn't as lonely as it appeared.

With her extra time, she decided to go water her largest lavender acreage and see if it had survived another night of voles. It was adjacent to the new neighbor's house, and maybe she'd get a chance to see who was moving in.

She watered and walked the perimeter of the corner lavender field. It was the one where the voles first took hold, and they had traveled through by tunneling underground. By the look of the trails and raised dirt, they were making a beeline for her kitchen garden.

She didn't see much more activity and was about to go back in after her chores. She carried her office phone, but there were no calls as yet. She realized she was on pins and needles about the Bonsine case. Jill figured the sheriff's department would do the raids in the very early morning. She was about to call Michelle to see if she'd heard anything when an older man appeared right at her fence line. A large dog was at his side. In the early morning light, with the sun behind him illuminating the edges of his full beard, he looked a little eerie. The surprise of it scared Jill for a minute. He was leaning on an ornate wooden cane.

"Hello," he said. He had a friendly and personable voice, and spoke very loudly. "I'm Sam Pardo, your new neighbor. Hope all that banging didn't get you up early. I told those moving guys not until eight, but they showed up early anyway."

"Not to worry," Jill said, "I could barely hear it. I'm Jill Wheaten. Welcome to this area. Are you and your family getting settled in?"

Sam looked down for a minute then looked up again as he spoke. "I'm fairly recently widowed," he said. "I'm here alone. It's been my dream to have some acreage. Don't know what I'll do with the land yet, but I'm enjoying buying all the toys that go along with farming these days."

Jill smiled. "This land is my dream too."

She looked closer at the animal. It was an old German shepherd dog, very gray around the muzzle and apparently well-mannered and trained. He sat sedately at Sam's side. Sam still hadn't made any comment on what she'd said about the land, but had looked down again and then off over the horizon. She followed his eyes, but there was nothing coming down the road. Sam suddenly looked tired. Now both he and the dog looked forlorn. There was no other word for it.

"Are you expecting someone?" she asked.

"My son was supposed to be here early, but I haven't seen him. He's coming from quite a way." Sam looked off for a few more moments, and then looked her way again.

"It's nice to have family," Jill commented. She needed to go get ready for work but wasn't sure how to take her leave. "You know, right now, I'm off to my job, but if you'd like to come over later tonight I'd be pleased to have you. You could meet the rest of my family."

Sam's face brightened. "That would be nice."

"I'll make a light dinner. I can clue you in about the area. How about six o'clock? Is that too early for you and…" She looked down at the dog.

"Grady."

"Nice name."

"Irene named her." Sam got that same wistful look on his face. "She's been gone six months. Died, you know." He caught himself and reverted back to that same cheerful demeanor she noticed at first. "Thanks for the dinner offer." He smiled broadly. "Oh, should I bring anything?"

"Just yourself and conversation," Jill said. "Bye, Sam, so glad I got to meet you on your first day here."

Jill was happy to have a new neighbor. She'd been afraid that house was going to be abandoned, since it was bank owned. If she had time she'd get an e-mail over to Maude and Roy, her neighbors on the other side of her property. She'd ask them to come over to meet Sam too. The best thing about being farther out in the country was that this old-fashioned friendliness was still in place.

Jill - Hospice Nurse, Book Two: Last Exit

On the walk back to her house, she thought about Sam. Six months after what she assumed was a lifetime partnership with someone wasn't time enough to even begin to know how to be, without that person. No wonder Sam looked so lonely. She never thought moving to a new area that soon after someone died was a good idea. For some, it seemed too painful being around the same surroundings where they'd lost their loved one. They tried to move to another area to help forget that life. Not to forget exactly, but to temper the pain. That kind of distraction was very temporary. People still had to process the grief.

Her mother was now awake, and Jill went in to dress and toilet her. Looking at her father's picture, always kept on her mom's dresser, she saw a young smiling man in uniform. She remembered that it wasn't until she was in junior high that she'd really understood what it meant to not have a father. It was a "dad and daughter" dance announcement. School administrations in those days didn't worry about being politically correct. She had no father to bring, or even someone to substitute as a father figure at the time, so she couldn't go. It hit her hard. She had known, but now she knew that she was fatherless. She was angry with her father for leaving her, for dying. It didn't make sense to her then. But in retrospect, it was the beginning of a normal period of grief.

Jill made a light breakfast. She had to feed her mom, slow spoonful by spoonful. Stina's appetite was off. Maybe it was part of a new stage she was slipping into. She sat her mom in an easy chair and turned on the morning news for her. She checked her e-mails. Then she sent off a brief invite to Maude and Roy, telling them they could meet their new neighbor Sam. She had a little time to spend looking on-line for ideas about hiring weekend help. She needed to call the dementia center and get on the respite wait list, as she realized she couldn't really wait that much longer. Jill didn't know why she hadn't looked into it before. The only thing she could think of is that in order to find the right solution you must be able to define the problem. Until Jason's job, and her knowing now that he might not choose a college near home, she'd skated by. She jotted down some telephone numbers from a caregiver's site and added a few of the agencies she knew from her job. She'd seen some of their workers and knew what type of person was needed. She had an advantage there.

As she got ready for work, she remembered she had a one-hundred-year-old's birthday party to attend. She dressed in a nice new set of brilliant blue lightweight scrubs and tied a colorful scarf around her neck.

She was still thinking about the new neighbor Sam, though. She decided that after she got to know him, and at an appropriate time, she might get some materials from Dean for Sam to read. If Irene had been under hospice care, Jill hoped it was a good death. For their sake, quite frankly as well as hers. Once people found out she was a hospice nurse, she was the recipient of all the information surrounding every death, and especially every hospice encounter in that person's history. Jill knew this was human nature, and ordinarily she liked the fact that they could tell their story. But she'd decided some time ago that for her own self preservation she had to be more judicious about letting people know what she did for a living.

Going back downstairs, she checked her mom again. Then she remembered about that call to Michelle. Michelle sounded sleepy when she answered.

"Jill," she remonstrated," It's hardly past seven o'clock for goodness sakes. I don't expect them to call us before eight."

"You don't?" Jill asked.

"No, Jill. Listen, they have to have that county guy with them, and he doesn't get to work until 7:30. Then the thing has to be coordinated. They don't want us even thinking about this until we're needed."

"Okay," Jill said, "I admit, I'm not experienced much in this. Well, I mean, I've never been in on a raid before. Where did you get your experience anyway?"

"Remember I told you about my internship, right out of college. The violently insane lockup unit. I showed you those big skeleton keys I had to carry around my waist on a belt like Nurse Ratched. Remember?"

"You didn't make that up?"

"Jill! I'm going back to bed. My alarm doesn't even go off for fifteen minutes. Oh, did you get your shoes?"

"Yes, and guess who was there at the bar?"

"Dano, just like I told him to be. Not that he needed any prompting."

"Michelle, please don't tell me you've stooped to matchmaking?"

"Goodbye, Jill."

Jill hung up smiling. With the team she worked with she could face another Friday.

She told Jason about the company for the evening meal and assured him it wouldn't be peanut butter and jelly. She took two vegetarian lasagnas out of the freezer to thaw in the refrigerator and checked that she had enough salad ingredients. Then she waved off her son with Stina in the back seat. Since her mom had started day care, she had been able to savor the few extra minutes she had in the morning. She sat with a hot cup of tea, allowing herself to relax for just a bit.

***

Work was tumultuous. The first thing Jill noticed was that Kim was crying. That was something she'd never seen before. Donna stood next to her and shooed everyone else away. Jill wondered if there was a connection with the celebration-cremation-roast. She hoped not. It was what the widow wanted. Then she wondered if it was still that headache thing. She'd seen Kim on the phone, speaking low, the past few days. Maybe Kim had heard some dire health news. Some doctors still did give bad news over the phone. It drove the hospice workers nutty, because they always had to sit through the telling of all those stories when they went out to sign on any new patients. Michelle was working with Stan to give another presentation to fellow doctors on how to break bad news. Jill was still mad that this wasn't taught at length in medical schools. It definitely made a difference if the families had the news given to them in a way they thought correct.

Stan had told the hospice workers he was making very slow progress in educating the doctors. It seemed to him that the newest doctors had better and better scientific and technical skills and worse and worse communication skills. It was hard to explain to them that there wasn't an easy or prescribed formula. It was just some ways were better than others, and you only had to look at the patient and family for a few clues to make the telling more humane. He said when he quizzed them on how to respond to the patient or family's request for conscious sedation and other buzzwords bantered around the Internet, they were at a loss of how to begin. Usually they pass that off on the hospice team, he'd said. Stan never said much, but when he did it was worth listening to.

Michelle still wasn't in yet, so Jill headed into Dean's office. It seemed he immediately sensed what she was there for. Of course he said nothing. Jill knew he knew part of what the problem was because Kim had told Jill she'd had to start getting some therapy sessions from someone Dean recommended. It seems all the deathbed confessions were weighing her down. As clergy, Kim had privacy privileges, of course. She told Jill that most things weighing on people's minds were small things from long ago. But over the years she'd heard enough of the occasional bigger things, and the therapist told her to let go of these stories or it would kill her. Kim had said the therapist was rather dramatic. "Like what kind of stories?" Jill had asked, just out of curiosity. She got the run down in response including: The hit and run accidents. The secret drinking or drug or financial disasters. The molestations. The horrendous battlefield experiences. The old or even current lovers. And, of course, the occasional decades old homicides! Honestly she didn't know how Kim did her job.

Dean looked very distressed himself. She didn't ask about Kim because even if he did know the full scoop, Jill didn't expect he'd ever be the one to spill the beans.

"You look tired, Dean."

"Jill, it's that funeral from yesterday."

"Lane's patient?"

"Yes, remember I'd done some pre-bereavement with the many grandchildren who lived in the home and were experiencing their first significant death. They asked me to come and help with the arrangements and then attend the funeral."

"How did it go?"

"I'd suggested to the adult children earlier that it might be a good idea to let the little ones bring something or write something for their grandmother to be included in the coffin. It seemed like a nice idea, and it's worked before. So after the main service and before the closing of the coffin, the grandchildren all took turns bringing their little memento up and placing it in their deceased grandma's hand or lap, or around her feet. Everyone was tearful and at first it worked fine. However, there were so many little ones and not all their mementoes were small. Soon, there was a mound! After everything was in, they could barely get the coffin closed."

"Oh, Dean," Jill empathized.

"That's not the worst part," Dean stated, and then he paused.

"It's not?"

Dean sighed and continued, "On the way to the open grave for the actual burial service, I realized that a small, thin piece of scarf, I think it was the one around a large teddy bear's neck, was sticking out of the backside of the coffin. You could barely see it, but it made a slight fluttering, right there outside the coffin."

"Oh my."

"I walked with my right arm up and my hand covering it all the way to the grave space, and then stood by it, in the same position, hoping no one else could see it, until the service was over. After everyone left but before the workmen lowered the woman into the ground, I pointed it out. They said they weren't allowed to touch anything. They were only authorized to turn the crank, lower the casket in, and then fill in with dirt. In order for the casket to be opened again at this point, it would practically call for an act of congress. And no, they said, they couldn't cut anything off either."

"Aww, Dean," Jill sympathized. "So do you think anyone else noticed that little piece of scarf?"

"No, apparently not. I got a call from the daughter after I got back in the office. She's the one who'd made most of the arrangements, and she thanked me. She said this was so important for the grandchildren. Said it made them feel part of the funeral. She reported that everyone in the family noted how reverent I was and how I kept my hand on the casket as a sign of respect. They said they'd never forget that. I won't either. I felt like the Dutch boy who had his finger in the dike. My shoulder is still aching."

"Dean, that was wonderful and the right thing to do." She reached out and put her hand on his shoulder, before remembering that was the sore side.

Dean winced and grabbed her hand. Shaking his head and smiling, he said, "Thanks, Jill…what a job we have."

Jill went back to the workroom and began her patient lineup. Everyone else was there now, but Kim and Donna were talking in the team conference room.

Michelle motioned Jill over. "Just got the call. They're in. I gave the sheriff's department the daughter's number. The spokesperson said they thought things were going smoothly. They'll call us if they need us."

"Okay," Jill said. She was relieved on the one hand, but on the other was feeling kind of left out. She went back over to her table next to Ron. She called and got on the respite list at the dementia center and put in another few calls to various agencies to see what the cost of hire was these days. She finally began to work on her schedule.

"Jill," Michelle asked as she passed by again, "I have the list of the amendments you need for your soil. I have a sample of a few of them too. I'll be out your way tonight. Is it okay if I drop them by?"

"Great," Jill answered. "I'm having my new neighbor over for dinner and you can join us…darn!"

"Huh?" Michelle asked.

"Oh, I just remembered that I took the frozen lasagnas out to thaw but forgot Jason won't be home since he works afternoons, so he can't get them started in the oven. Oh, well, we'll have salad and cheese toast. But come by."

"I will. Sounds good."

Lurline came by with some maps with various colored marker lines drawn. "I'm checking out territory boundaries for teams A and B in case Bill's serious about a new option for space. My eyes are getting crossed. I didn't major in geography."

"Actually I've decided I'm not even thinking about that move until the deal is done," Jill said.

"Wouldn't you know I got this assignment," Lurline complained. "I can't even read my map on the way to my patients half the time. Come to think of it, I don't even think Bill would know how to read a map. He always gives me the drudge work."

Ron looked up in sympathy. "You can do it, Lurline! Hey, look at this tie Dean lent me." He pulled out a new tie, still in its package, from his backpack. Do you think it goes with that suit I'm getting tailored?" It was a modest, purple print.

"Your suit was taupe? Good match. I think it looks nice," Jill said.

"Dean has good taste. You can trust it'll be right," Lurline added.

"Taupe? I thought the suit was brown. Anyway, Dean has written some lines for me for the funeral. Want to hear them?" he asked.

"This'll be good, I bet," Lurline said, smiling.

Ron cleared his throat, "Mr. Wedge was privileged to breathe this earth's atmosphere for seventy-three years."

"Uh…" Lurline stuttered.

"That's one of the lines Dean wrote?" Jill asked

"Elegant, huh?" Ron smiled. He had a twinkle in his eye though. "Ladies, I hope you know better than to think I'd say that. Most of the lines Dean wrote sounded too formal even for him. I think I'll talk about life being a ball game and Mr. Wedge knew the sport."

"Whew," Jill remarked.

"Just don't take that metaphor too far," Lurline warned. "Like that Vikings fan's funeral. One of Lane's first patients."

"Never heard that story," Jill said.

"They'd shrink-wrapped his casket with a Vikings logo. It was all the rage about a year ago. They just went bananas with all the sports stuff. Ended up some family members got in a fight with a few unruly Bears fans. Knocked the flower bier over and everything. That's why Lane doesn't like to go to funerals very much. She was traumatized."

Jill and Ron really laughed at that. So outrageous, and yet those sorts of things happened. Lane was so young and new to the field. That first funeral must have really scared her.

Michal Poe

Jill needed that good laugh, because Ron brought over his patient list and redistribution schedule for his expected time off. Jill saw that it was probably doable. One week was about the longest she could hold out though. It was good that Ron never took off more than one week at a time. That worked out well for Jill and the team. It seemed to refresh him. This way as he said, he could take time off more often around his son's school holidays, rather than the full four weeks in one shot. Jill had never taken her four weeks consecutively, but she always thought she would one day. Right now, she didn't know how people could be away from this kind of a job for that long a period of time. Donna had done that once and the whole office fell apart. Although Donna looked well rested when she returned, she said she'd never do it again. It took her three months to get things back in order.

***

It was already time for morning team meeting. Once again the workers filed in and found their places. Kim, still red-eyed, tried to look pleasant but was not succeeding. Trying to smile through tears put a terrible grimace upon her face. Donna caught Jill's eye and gave a little smile. Jill then knew Donna had things under control.

While they waited for Bill, Dean pulled out a few small tealight candles. He inserted them into a small brass receptacle as he explained. "My idea is to have a consistent little ceremony after we discuss those patients who have died since we last met. After a prayer or saying, which Kim has always provided, we'll have a short moment of silence to honor their passing. Then I'll gently blow them out. I know they used to do it here many years ago. This is a very healing process, it takes but a few moments, and the literature shows this commemoration is very meaningful."

"Oh, I like that," Lane said.

Everyone else nodded in agreement. Dean appeared pleased his idea was so readily accepted and appreciated.

To save time, and while still waiting for their boss to arrive, Jill let the group know that Adele Fromm's death went well.

Dean added that he'd called Frank, who had surprisingly accepted the idea of grief counseling and, since his son was going to stay with him for a time, they made an appointment to see Dean in the hospice office sometime next week. He also said, "Rita's widower, Davis, is very open to counsel."

Lane reported that one of her patients had an uneventful expected death as well. Thursday had been a busy day.

Kim quietly passed her reading over to Dean, who understood she wanted him to read it. Dean lit the candles, and read a lovely passage about life's journey and how some were able to approach their final days with a peaceful heart. Toward the end of the short reading, it emphasized how faith decreed your hopes. In the beautiful candlelight the moment of quiet began.

It began peacefully, but then the ceremony was spoiled by Bill's interruption. He'd suddenly burst through the door, scattering paperwork and hurried, no, he actually ran over to the table and blew out the candles.

"Staff! People!" he loudly lamented. "Do you understand how these flames could set off an alarm, send out the fire department, and impugn my spotless record of following the CRCs of this building?"

"You moved quick as a bunny," Sandy exclaimed.

Michal Poe

No one could comment on Bill's act or Sandy's exclamation. They sat in silence, looking at the small trails of smoke emitted from the extinguished candles.

Bill grunted but did not break his busy-ness. He gathered up a few dropped packets and sent around data sheets to be initialed by each field staff member. It showed their production statistics.

"Before we begin, I need to let you know how our accountability issue is proceeding. I had the expert look over all the data late last night and she noted how your points all add up to more than expected, so she's sure to get her bonus. I reviewed these same numbers this morning, and by comparison with our old method, I noted that if anything, you have been seeing slightly less than your usual load of patients. The consultant will be paid for this week, as that was the prior commitment, but I have let her go. We will go back to the usual method starting Monday. Please initial that sheet I passed out to everyone and send it back this way."

Without any comment from the staff, Bill waited to begin gathering back the initialed production data list.

The staff looked over their own sheets. Leaning over, Jill saw Ron was taking an extra second to write a note, after his initials. "I'm sorry to see this new method go, it helped me keep track of my actual work load each day." Seeing that, Jill added her own comment, and then everyone at the table seemed to follow his lead and wrote a nice comment about the production sheets. They surprised themselves by acknowledging the method's usefulness. The days would fly by so suddenly that by the end of the week you weren't sure what you'd accomplished, but the sheet showed. It was uplifting.

Jill - Hospice Nurse, Book Two: Last Exit

Bill waited impatiently for his papers. He tapped his foot and checked his watch.

Ron surreptitiously wrote a note to Jill on the back of a scrap note sheet and passed it to her under the table. It said, "Man, I'm sorry he caught on so soon." Jill smiled as she tore the note into teeny, tiny, little pieces and stuck it in the front pocket of her scrubs.

Bill, having finished his mayhem, went on to his next point in a calmer mood. "Lurline, have you had time to look over the map allotments?" he asked.

"Yes, sir," Lurline answered. "I can tell you this: an important issue is finding a more central location for our office in order to make the areas and travel times fair."

"I think the word you meant, Lurline, was equitable. And, I'm always saddened to see how the issue of fairness is continually presented. In this field I would think sacrifice would be the more expected mode," Bill pontificated. "In this economy there must be plenty of large, good spaces that are less expensive." He continued, "Donna, what about your search for appropriate accommodations?"

Sandy interjected, "We gotta get a bigger space to hire more nurses and especially more home health aides. Everybody wants a bath every day. I'm worn to the bone."

Donna nodded toward Sandy to let her know she'd heard, and then spoke directly to Bill.

"Most of the places I visited with our site finder, Mr. Ames, were even farther out or were of less square footage than we currently lease. The most appropriate-looking one had drainage problems. Nothing acceptable as yet. I'm beginning to think that building our own space from the bottom up and really fitting our growth needs would be a more fitting solution."

Jill was surprised by that comment, as just yesterday Donna had mentioned to Jill that there was a pretty good space she'd seen the day before. She figured Donna was planting a seed. So skillful, Jill thought. Maybe I should use her as a sales consultant with my truck farm ideas.

"Drainage problems?" Bill inquired.

"Flies," Donna answered. "Used to be a dairy."

"No bugs. I refuse," commented Sandy.

"Let's keep at it, Donna," Bill said, and then as if to further spur her on he added, "The Eco-team is on my back, thinking there might be asbestos in the ceilings here."

"What?" Sandy practically yelled. "Bad enough we go into these old homes with mold and every other thing, we don't need to be poisoned here."

"Sandy!" Bill replied, raising his voice, "I will keep you informed, and I'll protect my staff at any cost."

Donna, noticing some looks at the table after Bill used the words, *at any cost*, stated, "All the more reason for us to find a solution quickly, Bill."

"Quite right," Dean said.

"Yes," Bill admonished. "Not a word or rumor about what might not even be a problem. I'm sorry I mentioned it. I forgot some of us jump to conclusions with alarming regularity." He looked around the room for emphasis. "Surely we can find as much space at even a lower cost if we put our nose to the grindstone."

That comment reminded them they needed to get busy with the meeting. They reviewed their patients, their schedules, and their expected times and ran current treatment plans by the medical director.

Stan was still munching on the morning's repast, mainly leftover chicken wings and garlic bread from one of the many weekday parties Lane gave or attended. The doctor hadn't joined in the earlier discussion, and not because he was eating either. His usual place of work was several buildings away at a small medical center. The only time he was in the building was at morning team. Through the years Jill noticed he wisely chose his battles with Bill. He definitely stuck to his medical issues unless there was some staff issue he could influence. He was a champion to the nurses, always available and always courteous. Jill was on the cusp of speaking to him about his hearing problem, though, because the nurses were becoming more and more aware of how that could be a real issue.

Bill apparently remembered that he'd heard about Dean's research regarding conflict resolution.

"Team," he said, "I'm sure you don't mind me holding forth on another subject, I want to let you know that Dean's work this week with the volunteers has resulted in a new theory. This has not gone unnoticed. Congratulations, Dean."

Dean looked more than a little embarrassed and gave a weak smile. "Thank you."

He couldn't muster much more, Jill figured, because she heard he'd already been informed by Donna that Bill had decided that Community Hospice and, more importantly, Bill's name should be on the paper as well. Dean had told Donna he didn't know how he was going to handle that.

They were finally about finished with the patient list when Michelle and Jill were beeped by the sheriff's department and had to leave regarding the adult abuse case.

Michal Poe

***

They left together in Michelle's vehicle. They were asked to go to the Bonsine daughter's home. They were to check out and console Mrs. Bonsine, while Cherie, the daughter, was to head back to pick up the necessary medicines, supplies, and paperwork from the home. Michelle picked up her complete message and then explained what had happened as she drove. The workers at the chop shop had been quietly rounded up. The son however, had apparently been tipped off before the authorities arrived and had escaped in the meat truck. No one thought he'd get too far, especially since they had a full description and the license number. They did believe the meat sign had been painted over. The sad thing, Michelle explained, was what was found when the social worker from the county met the daughter, Cherie, and they were about to go into the home together. Mary Bonsine was crying while frantically trying to open the many locks. When she heard someone outside, she begged someone to call 911. They did. The fire department had to break the door down, and Mr. Bonsine was found dead in his chair. The ambulance people told the sheriff the man had been dead for some time, several hours at least. It looked like a natural death, but since he was not currently under a doctor's care there would be an autopsy. Besides, the whole place was now a crime scene, due to the son's "business." Cherie had gladly taken her mom home with her. Mary hadn't been informed about her son's getaway and law problem. She may have known it in her heart, but everyone thought it wasn't necessary to reveal all that at this time. It was enough that she had to deal with her spouse's death.

Jill - Hospice Nurse, Book Two: Last Exit

Jill was sick about the whole thing. Jill figured Mr. Bonsine had died of pneumonia or heart attack based on her observations on Thursday, less than twenty-four hours ago. It was another case of the caregiver dying before the patient. Jill had seen this happen so many times. The stress, the strain, and the lack of self-care, either a previous trait or a new one, contributed to worsening health conditions. This was especially true for elderly caregivers. Maybe she should have called an ambulance when she was there on Thursday. But Mr. Bonsine had refused treatment, and there was no use in second-guessing.

Things went well at Cherie's home. While Jill talked with Cherie, Michelle was able to assess Mary's emotional state. She gave Cherie and Jill her findings. Things were relatively calm for now, despite that morning's shock for all of them. Cherie was told Dean was available to come out and help the daughter break any further news about the son, and probably that would be needed. Jill did her physical assessment on Mary and then called Mary's doctor and got her a prescription for a light sedative. Cherie agreed to have daily nursing visits for her mom until things further settled down. A volunteer was on her way to sit with Mary until the daughter could get back with the medicines and whatever personal things the county would allow her to remove from the now cordoned-off home.

When they left Cherie's house, it was not even ten o'clock, yet Jill admitted she was exhausted. Michelle pulled through a drive-through coffeehouse and bought Jill a hot tea.

"Jill," Michelle started, "You did a good job with the Bonsines. As good as anyone could."

"I know…but," Jill said quietly.
"Nobody failed nobody."
"No?"
"No."

Jill took a deep breath. She looked over at Michelle. "Thank you, friend."

They headed over to the Coultrans. This was to be the co-visit about the intimacy issues. They needed to see how that "sex talk" thing had turned out.

On their way, Michelle asked, "Jill, do you know what's making Kim cry?"

"No. But I do know Donna is helping. And, since Donna is involved we can hope for a good outcome."

"I think she's working on Bill's head about this one," Michelle said. "At team, after she was talking about locations, she sneaked a peek at Kim."

"Snuck."
"Sneaked."
"Snuck."

∗∗∗

Their banter ended and they drove the rest of the way in blessed silence. When they arrived at the Coultrans', they found Mrs. Coultran, Stevie, asleep in the front porch swing.

Jill and Michelle stood on the porch. They didn't want to startle her, but it didn't seem very safe to be sleeping outside like that. It was such a busy street.

"Ahem," Jill coughed.

Stevie opened one eye. "Oh, good, you're here."

"You looked like you were resting well," Michelle ventured.

"Yes, for a few hours," Stevie answered. "I tell you, this morning I was red-eyed, aching, exhausted. I had to haul the trash out to the curb. When I leaned over the can to adjust the lid, my upper body's weight was supported, and I think I fell asleep."

"No!" Jill exclaimed.

"I must have been beyond description, embarrassingly tired. Later, on the phone with your home bathing aide, I became confused when giving directions to the house. She's coming this afternoon to start the bathing service, you know. Anyway, I hung up pretending the line had been cut. I had to collect my thoughts before she rang back."

"I'm so sorry," Michelle said.

"That's not the worst of it," Stevie continued. "When I was giving Dan his morning pills, I came close to seriously mixing up the doses. I needed rest. I've been at my wit's end lately. I went to the garage, pushed back the driver's seat to snooze there, but realized I couldn't hear if Dan called me. And then I thought, maybe someone would think I was trying to do myself in or something."

"Aw," Jill said to further Stevie's words.

"Well, I came out here with an old quilt, and I tell you, sleeping in the fresh air is wonderful. I feel great."

Needing to get to the issue at hand, Michelle asked, "Are you tired because of what we talked about yesterday?"

"No," Stevie replied. "After that talk he came to me and apologized. He said he was being selfish. He was really sweet about it. I've just been bone tired."

"So you think you were overdoing it? Working too hard?" Michelle queried.

"Yes, I've been short and crabby with him and everyone, including you guys. I've been keeping myself busy with so many trivial things. I mean the dusting can wait, right?"

"Forever," Jill said.

"Floors too," Michelle added.

"Right. As I was dozing off, I was thinking, I'm not only going to get that bathing person for Dan, I'll get that volunteer, hired help, the works!" Stevie exclaimed. "I'll spend more time with Dan. You know, I realized that's all he really wanted anyway. Just to have my attention."

"Good conclusion," Michelle stated.

"Very wise," Jill said.

After a brief checkup on Dan, Michelle drove Jill back to the office so she could pick up her car and finish her visits for the day.

"Hey," Michelle said as Jill transferred her nursing bags into her Jeep parked in the side parking lot. "I'm closing the designated problem—intimacy issues. So close it on your paperwork too, okay?"

"Okay. What are you going to put as the solution on the treatment plan?"

"Not sexy lingerie. Not that instructional *Positions for Comfort* DVD. Not little purple pills."

"Seriously, Michelle, how should I word the solution?"

"Write: *Caregiver allowing additional help in the home.*"

***

Jill, on her way to the noon birthday party visit scheduled with the McCarthys, used the time to call Fern to check on Stina. Fern reported that Stina, although a little more listless than usual, appeared okay.

"Will you let me know if she doesn't have an appetite for lunch?" Jill requested. "She didn't eat too much for breakfast."

"Oh," Fern responded, "we fed her a little early and put her to bed for her afternoon nap already."

"Well, call me if you need me there for anything," Jill insisted.

Jill felt a little better about the situation. Managing her mom's care while working put her in the same mindset as when Jason was a small child and couldn't report how he'd been during the day. She trusted Fern, and Jill realized, once again, that she needed to assure herself that this was the best situation for her mom. She didn't need to add more guilt upon the circumstances she had no control over…a lesson Michelle had stressed only a short time ago. If she couldn't let go, she'd end up as burdened as Kim was before she learned to loosen her feelings of distress over some of her patients' secrets.

Jill would be able to get to the nudist's place early enough to assess Harry and have some time to socialize. That extra time she'd call her lunch. She was glad she'd chosen her newest, shortest sleeved, light cotton scrubs so as not to be overdressed and way too warm for the dayroom.

When she drove up, the guard at the gate was eating birthday cake.

"I didn't miss the party, did I?" Jill asked.

"McCarthy's? No. This is from the Leeds. There's a birthday every day around here. Good thing everybody's always in their birthday suit." He laughed heartily at his own joke.

Jill drove into the complex, parked, and found the party.

"Life, you just can't beat it," Harry McCarthy noted while looking over the festivities, after Jill finished her quick nursing assessment. Jill agreed. Thank heavens her job wasn't death and disaster everyday, all day.

Harry's mom, Effie, was a kick. She stayed clothed though. She and Jill were the only ones who looked normal, because a silly little birthday hat on all those naked people looked more comical than words could describe.

There was a small buffet. Jill noted it was mostly raw and dehydrated foods. Harry and Linda must have hired a special caterer. The dehydrated corn tortillas were good, even without the salt. She decided she'd like to get the recipe for the raw vegetarian Swedish meatballs. But she was especially interested in the natural dairy-free chocolate. It was delicious—now that's the kind of raw food she could endorse.

Harry tapped on his water glass. "Everyone," he announced, "I want to give my mother a chance to tell us all what's kept her so healthy and lively all these one hundred years."

Effie, in her wheelchair, took a microphone from the man recording the event and in a surprisingly strong voice, proclaimed, "One way to get old is to keep having birthdays." She paused to let the laughter die down a little.

Jill saw Harry was beaming as he sat proudly at his mother's side.

"I've eaten and drank what I wanted when I wanted it," Effie continued. "Mainly bananas, oatmeal, pork chops, and lemon ices. Not mixed together, of course. I never missed a chance to have fun. Most importantly, I let all problems go—since I couldn't do much about them anyway. That's all my wisdom. Oh, and remember to try and make the most of every minute, live for today, because you may not get one hundred years."

There was a moment of silence as everyone digested that good bit of advice. Soon, the champagne (really sparkling apple juice) toasts began. "Happy Birthday" was sung and the carrot cake was cut. Jill sat back and thoroughly enjoyed herself.

Effie motioned for Jill to come near.

Jill pulled a chair directly in front of her so they could hear one another over the festivities.

"Thank you," Effie said with sincerity. "So many thanks for taking good care of my son."

"You're welcome," Jill answered. "It is my pleasure."

"Who'd have thought I'd outlive all my children," Effie added with misted eyes. Then, as if to change to a lighter subject, she added, "I don't know how these people stand it with no clothes, it's very cool in here."

Jill, who thought the opposite, took the colorful silk scarf she'd carefully picked out that morning from around her neck and draped it over Effie's shoulders.

"Happy birthday, Effie."

Effie smiled and fingered the soft scarf. When she glanced back up, Jill was still looking at her and Effie smiled again, glowing with true joy.

"Only got today, as I said. I'd better live by my own wise words."

When it was about time to go, Harry commented that he'd forgotten to order the confetti. Jill pulled the tiny bits of paper out of her scrubs pocket. It was the note she'd torn up from Ron at morning meeting, and now she threw the little pieces of paper into the air. Everyone laughed.

Jill left feeling so good about life in general. She chuckled as she got back in the car. She was going to write down Effie's advice. She must have needed that lesson today, because Effie's statement about letting the problems that you had no control over go was especially propitious.

Michal Poe

She thought about the part of Effie's speech where she reported that she ate what she wanted when she wanted. She might use that as an example with some of the families she dealt with. During her first year as a hospice nurse, Jill always advised her hospice patients who were nearing death to eat whatever they wanted and could tolerate. But she soon found that unless the patient was over eighty years of age or so, most hospice families seemed very intent on providing a healthy diet. Jill soon realized it was because even though no one could help stay the disease, at least the food was something that could be controlled.

Jill picked up a few messages from her phone as she was driving to her last appointment. Fortunately there were no emergencies. She got a cryptic message from Donna saying, "Problem practically solved—no more tears." Jill knew she was talking about Kim, and Jill was anxious to get into the office and get the details. Aside from the Sealys, and oh how she hoped their hallway stayed clear, she was asked by Ron to stop by Chase Miller's in the late afternoon. He said they had a little surprise. Jill was glad she'd have the time. This giving back was important for the patients and their families. She hoped the surprise wasn't anything extravagant though.

Additionally, Ron left her word that he couldn't keep that snake anymore because Tammy was having a fit about it. Also, his son was creeped out when he found out that the snake ate live mice. Everyone was to be on the lookout to find Mr. Slithers a home.

The last message was from Jason, asking if he could bring Sherrice's dad to the dinner that night. He said that according to Sherrice, Rob had been lonely and at loose ends ever since the divorce. Although Jill thought it was a nice idea and thoughtful of Jason to ask, her little get-together was becoming quite an event. She did need to officially meet Rob though. Maybe she'd see how Rob might help Jason, as long as he didn't overstep his boundaries. She returned the message giving the okay. She'd have to stop by and get a dessert on her way home. Carrot cake sounded very good. Lemon ice too. Stina used to make that with fresh lemon, lots of sugar, and pulverized ice. When it came to food, Jill's head was easily turned.

***

The Sealys' home, so normal and serene from the outside, was the usual turmoil inside. The hallway had become partially re-cluttered, and on top of that, Len Sealy had acquired a cat, a vicious-looking tawny yellow tomcat they'd named Honey-Pot. Even without its torn up ears, it would have been quite the specimen. Ordinarily, Jill was not afraid of cats. True, she had allergies, but only to long-haired cats, and this was a short-haired domestic. It stood on Joyce's bed and hissed and spat at her.

"Isn't that wonderful!" Len exclaimed. "Little Doggie Bone is not a good watch dog, but this cat is so protective of Joyce you'd think we'd had him for years."

It was with great difficulty that Jill persuaded Len to remove the cat so she could begin her regular assessment. Joyce appeared more somnolent than before, and Jill needed to find out what was different.

She found the problem. It appeared Joyce was narcotized. She called Len over and they reviewed the medicine schedule.

"Oh, I thought I was supposed to give her that pain pill every time she ate. Just only morning and night you say?" Len asked.

"Yes. I don't think the few extra you've given her have done any real harm. I'll call the doctor to see what he thinks. I'll leave her medicine list here with the amounts and times to administer, and you check it off when she takes things. Is that okay?"

"I hope you're not mad at me," a crumpled Len said dolefully.

"No," Jill quickly responded. "Let's just take this precaution."

"It's hard to keep track, what with all the animals and all."

"This will make it easier. And," Jill added, "Len, have you given any thought to keeping the animal population down a little?"

"Yes, Joyce and I talked about it yesterday. That's why we didn't take in those rabbits a neighbor brought over yesterday. He said if we didn't take them, he'd eat 'em. Just about broke Joyce's heart."

"That's terrible."

"He was just bluffing, but still…"

Jill shook her head and patted Len's arm. She didn't ask about how they'd acquired the cat. She didn't want to hear any more sad stories today if she could help it. At least the cat had a happy ending.

Len brightened up and pinned the medication sheet right above Joyce's bed. "That way it will stay safe and I can always check it."

"Good thinking," Jill encouraged.

Jill's call to the doctor revealed Joyce would probably sleep for the rest of the day, but no harm expected due to just two extra doses of the medicine. Jill was glad Joyce had been on her schedule today. If the visit had had to wait until Monday, it would have been a serious problem.

Jill finished and realized she would have the few extra minutes it would take to stop by Chase's house to see what the surprise was. On the way there, she phoned Fern since she hadn't heard about how her mom was doing this afternoon.

"Hard to say, because she can't really tell me," Fern volunteered. "I have to read her actions, but I don't really see anything amiss there."

"Thanks," Jill said. "We'll bring her home at the usual time then."

Jill answered a few calls from various agencies. She would start interviewing for weekend help next week, after her work hours.

***

At the Miller house, no one answered the door again. She saw Ron's motorcycle in the driveway, so she went around the side of the house as she'd done before. As she was closing the gate, she looked back over her shoulder because she heard something near her Jeep. She saw two policemen getting out of their patrol car. Her heart sank, wondering if perhaps Chase had died and his mom had called 911.

She hurried through to the backyard. But no, everyone looked fine. Even though it was still broad daylight, roaring flames were coming out of the fire pit. Chase was in a lounge chair, pulled up near the fire and covered in a light blanket. A tent was pitched farther back in the grassy area. Ron, Chase, and all his friends were roasting potatoes and corn in the fire. Several hot dogs on sticks were propped over the fire too. Bags of marshmallows were in abundance.

Michal Poe

The two policemen were now right behind her.

"Hi Ron," Jill called out. "These gentlemen drove up right after me." She motioned in the direction of the officers. She didn't want anyone to think she'd brought the law.

The policemen were surveying the scene as they neared the campfire. It was all very quiet now.

Ron stood up and walked toward Jill, and then Chase's dad came out of the back door and walked over to the group.

One of the policemen very politely said, "Sorry to bother you, but we've had reports of explosions from your backyard."

One of Chase's friends in the group smiled sheepishly. "We did let off a few fireworks earlier," he admitted. "Sorry, we weren't thinking about the noise."

Mr. Miller explained to the policemen, "It's kind of a last gift my wife and I are giving to my son. He's pretty ill. These are two of his hospice nurses here." He pointed to Jill and Ron.

The policemen smiled, obviously relieved to find no real concerns. They seemed in no hurry to leave. They even accepted the suggestion, from Chase, to stay a while and cook up a s'more.

Jill stayed for a short while. Mr. Miller told her and Ron that Chase had let him know that after he died—and this time Mr. Miller said that phrase without choking up—Chase wanted Ron to have his weightlifting set and Jill could have his laptop computer since she'd helped his mom so much.

Mr. Miller saw Jill's hesitation and said, "Ron told me about the one-hundred-dollar limit; these things are used and are not worth over that."

Ron gave a broad smile. "Thanks," he said. "That's excellent!"

Jill followed his lead and gave her own thanks, but it was hard to be gracious in these situations. She had to try reminding people more that the gift they gave by letting the nurses into their lives was plenty already.

***

Back at the office, Jill did her best to wrap up her day. She overheard Lane on the phone trying to get an emergency appointment with her esthetician for a facial. Donna heard too and said, "Lane, tonight at that studio they'll put so much pancake makeup on you nobody could even begin to see your pores."

The office cleared out, but before Jill left she had to go by Donna's desk and wish her good luck on the panel that evening. She did that and then hesitantly broached her worry. "Donna, about Kim…"

"All problems solved," Donna assured. "Kim's been crying because her spouse lost his job with the architecture firm due to downsizing and didn't have a project in the works in his private consultation firm."

"Oh, no. It's no wonder she's been so upset."

"Worse than that. Kim said Brent was considering uprooting the whole family and taking this job offer down south."

"That is worse."

"I solved two problems with one strategy, though."

"This I've got to hear."

"Papers are being drawn up for Brent's architectural business to build a large complex for Community Hospice. A design that will put this business on the map, as Bill put it. Seems we may get even with the new vets program. Bill has donors who are willing to contribute, and he's pretty excited. There'll be room for auxiliary services, community educational classes, hospice RN certifications, and everything we've wanted. Possibly even a small in-house hospice unit for those who have no other living arrangements."

"No way."

"Yes way. And the location is not in this out-of-the-way burb, but in midtown on one of those big infill lots."

"I don't know how you did it. I'm flabbergasted!" Jill said.

"The papers aren't completed, but there are very few glitches that haven't been thought through. There's even room for parking," Donna said as she straightened up her desk to prepare to leave. "I've been working on this for a while, but Kim's concern and the move and all put me in high gear. I planted seeds. I weeded. I nurtured. There'll be a nice harvest." Donna looked across at Jill and added, "You're not the only one who gardens."

"You're definitely in the right field, Donna." Jill laughed a little at her own wordplay.

"Thank you, dear," Donna said. "Compliment received."

"How soon might all this magic take place?"

"Should be built and ready for move-in by the first of next year. Quicker if Bill has his way."

Jill continued to shake her head in amazement most of the way home. It was Friday again, the week had wrapped up fairly well, and she had her second wind looking forward to the evening and the weekend as well. Especially since she was going to rearrange her mom's environment to make it more suitable for her care. She would keep the baby monitor near her mom's bed, though. She needed to be able to hear what was going on throughout the night. If C.J. wanted to buy something else for their mom, she'd suggest some good baby gates.

She stopped and picked up a three-layer carrot cake and some fresh mint leaves for the lemon ices. Something had dug around her mint plants, so she currently didn't have much, but Jill wasn't too worried about that because mint propagated so quickly. The lemons were plentiful on her two lemon trees. Many of them were still on the tree from early spring. She was a little worried about dinner though. With Michelle coming, her new neighbor Sam, the other neighbors, her mom, Jason's girlfriend, and now Sherrice's dad, that would make an impromptu dinner for nine. She could handle that though. Things were looking up.

***

The first thing Jill did after returning home was to check her mom for a fever. But Stina seemed the same as usual. Jason told her that Fern had reported no real changes, and Stina had responded as usual during the late afternoon. Once again, Jill had worried over nothing.

Jill gathered the lemons, then she sat her mom at the small table in the kitchen while she made a large salad and set out cookie tins with bread, which she topped with grated cheese, ready to pop into the oven. Stina was fondling the peapods that Jill was going to include in the salad. Jill remembered the many times she and her mother would shell peas from the garden. While Stina ate one of the raw pods, Jill caught her eye and Stina seemed to recognize Jill for an instant. Whenever Jill saw that glimmer it pleased her so, even though it tore at her heart. It was a wonderful and unexpected gift after her concerns about her mom over the day.

Michal Poe

Jason arrived with Sherrice. Rob was coming later, Jason reported. Jill left them in the kitchen with Stina and, after changing into white cotton capris and a red sleeveless top, she walked around her property. Checking the area she'd been in that morning, she was shocked to see not only evidence of voles but also many dug up areas, large holes really. Then she saw Grady. Dirt was flying. For an old dog he certainly looked athletic. He was so busy he didn't notice Jill. Her heart sank. A new neighbor, and already a problem… how long would it take before she could get an adequate fence up, and at what added expense?

She called Grady to her and clapped her hands. He didn't seem to hear. She walked closer and whistled loudly. Her turned and came to her. He didn't jump up, but docilely licked her hands and wagged his tail. She walked him back over to his own territory.

Sam answered the door.

"Jill, am I late for dinner already?"

"No, but your dog was over to my place and I didn't want you to worry if you couldn't find him." She just couldn't let Sam know the damage the dog had done, not until she thought about it further anyway.

"Thanks," Sam replied. "Let me get my cane and I'll walk you back." Then he added, "Whoa, Grady you're a dirty mess. Look at you, no one would ever know you have bad arthritis."

"He's getting around really well."

"He's so happy and lively, it looks like this fresh country air is agreeing with him already."

"Let me get your leash and I'll walk him." Jill suggested. She didn't want to stop by the digging area and maybe have

Grady decide to have another chance at the voles. "We'll go on the road," Jill suggested to Sam as she snapped the leash on the dog, "that way he won't accidentally get wild and run too far away."

"Now that's just plain thoughtful." Sam smiled.

Jill, Sam, and Grady slowly walked back to Jill's home. She explained about her mother's illness so Sam would be prepared. Sam explained that his son could only stay a couple of hours that morning, otherwise he'd be with them too. Jill pointed out where her neighbors Maude and Roy lived. Just then, she saw them walking down the road toward her house. At the mailbox, Jill made introductions. Maude had brought chocolate oatmeal cookies. She loved to bake and usually came with a pastry in hand. A strange car was in the driveway, and a tall, heavyset man on the porch stopped knocking and turned toward the group coming up the drive.

Jill figured that must be Rob. He carried a bottle of red wine. "Sherrice told me lasagna, so I brought red wine. Is that okay?" he inquired.

"Absolutely," Jill answered. She didn't have the heart to tell him the menu had changed.

Grady was ensconced in the fenced backyard and immediately laid down in the tall, cool grass. It was clear to Jill he was more than a little tired from his enthusiastic efforts in her garden.

Jill knew she'd have to explain the shortened menu later, but in the meantime she put out the nuts, crackers and raw veggies, while Rob poured the wine. Jill pulverized some ice and made lemon ice for herself, Stina, Jason, and Sherrice.

Sam heard the nightly news playing in the background and leaned his ear toward the TV. Jill brought him over and introduced him to her mom. Sam seemed to have a strange reaction, as he stared at Stina with an open mouth for a few seconds. Then he caught himself and sat in a club chair next to her recliner.

Taking her hand, he asked, "Hello there. May I watch the news with you?"

Stina momentarily took notice of him before the confused look came back. But first she'd shaken her head yes as she looked back at the TV. If Jill didn't know better, it seemed her mother understood the question. Sam looked very happy to have someone with whom he could watch the news. Jill left them there.

Jill put the cheese bread in the oven. She was about to go join her other guests when Rob popped into the kitchen. He was a smiley, gregarious man, and Jill certainly could believe he'd done well in car sales. He stood a little too close. In an effort to be extra friendly, Jill asked him a few open-ended questions, and being a true quidnunc, he immediately gave her tons of unwarranted advice. He never stopped to take a breath as Jill, his quarried prey, hurriedly finished her tasks. She was able to smile and escape to join her other guests, but Rob was right at her heels.

Sherrice looked a little concerned when Jill and Rob exited the kitchen together. She apparently knew her dad's overbearing tendencies. Smiling, she said, "Come here, dad, look at these pictures of Jason as a little boy."

Jill was relieved that Sherrice was so perceptive. That intelligent girl, with her sweet, unassuming manner, was revealing a maturity well beyond her years.

Looking around and finding her house full gave Jill a kind of contentment. She decided she'd have to have a little Friday night get-together at least once a month. Usually on Friday nights she didn't do any farming anyway and just wanted to rest up from her week. The company was nice.

Hearing Michelle's pickup in her gravel drive, she went to the porch to meet her. Michelle was with someone else who was getting out on the passenger side. Dano?

Coming up the walk, Dano looked a little embarrassed. He carried two large, foil-covered casseroles. Out of context, out of the bar, Jill found it hard to register what she was seeing.

Michelle explained in her greeting, "Jill, you told me cheese toast for guests. Well, I was talking to Dano around lunch time and he said he had a killer recipe from his mom for lasagna."

Jill looked at Dano. He wore jeans and an open-necked light blue shirt. It looked like he had muscles. She hadn't noticed so many before. He was pale, though, probably didn't get out in the sun much.

"Hope you don't mind my tagging along," he stated in an almost shy way.

Jill thought he seemed so different, in another agreeable way, out of his usual element.

"How could I refuse a guest carrying the homemade dinner?" Jill said.

Dinner was splendid. The lasagna was the richest, best dish she'd had for ages. Dano generously served from the beautiful, deep ceramic dishes. Stina was quiet and not able to feed herself, so Jason had been helping his grandma eat as he sat on one side of her. But then Sam, who appeared to love his reprised role as caregiver, began pinching off bits of cheese toast for her. It seemed natural. Jill didn't know what to think. No one else seemed to notice.

Michal Poe

Jill talked about her farming and hinted she'd have to fence the back acreage of the property. Roy said he was looking into the newer, longer-range electric periphery fences. Michelle had recently fenced part of her land and said she had the name of someone good who could do it cheap.

Then the topic went to the voles, and Maude said, "I hope those critters find enough sustenance on your land so they won't head on over our way!"

Dano looked over at Jill, "Remember, my dog is good at chasing down vermin."

Sam diverted his attention from Stina long enough to say maybe his dog could help too, if he wasn't so old.

Rob insisted that there was nothing better than snakes for those pests. Jill briefly thought of Mr. Slithers's need for a new home and decided she would inquire when the time was right if Rob was interested in a new pet. Rob wasn't quite so overly talkative in the larger group.

Dano seemed to look at Jill a lot, but not directly, almost peeking at her, and if that wasn't sweet, she didn't know what was.

Jason and Sherrice seemed comfortable in the company of all the older people at the table.

Michelle went to her pickup truck after dinner and brought the soil amendment materials up onto the porch. Everyone took their carrot cake and Maude's homemade cookies out there and found space in the chairs or on the steps.

Sam wanted to help Stina with her cake.

"I'm good at this, Jill." He said, smiling. "Small bites. That's the trick."

Jill had planned to tune into the hospice panel, scheduled on the local station at 7:30, but she suddenly realized she'd missed it. Work seemed very far away. Donna would handle things well.

"Jill," Dano asked, "Do you mind if I go smoke out on that side of the yard?"

"Of course not," she answered. "There's a bench under that big tree over there," she pointed.

"The sycamore?"

"Yes," Jill answered, rather surprised that he knew the type of tree it was. He must not have always been such an indoor person. She loved that tree because it didn't take any care and provided shade for her whole yard. The previous owners had told her they had planted it when their son was a baby. That was forty years ago. Jill hoped she could have another 40 years on this land.

Later, she looked at him standing out there with his cigar, looking over her yard and plantings. She briefly considered walking over to where he stood, but as it was, she could faintly smell the cigar smoke from the porch. She was fairly interested in Dano, and he was obviously interested in her. Even without Michelle's transparent little cupid intervention this evening, Jill could see she'd like to get to know him better. No rush though. Everything seemed so calm, so natural.

Jill was happy. Even with her many cares and concerns, tonight was special, the start of the new, more social Jill. A whole weekend to look forward to and no problems that couldn't be fixed with a little finesse. She knew it would take less effort to unravel her concerns than the time and thought she took with any one of her patients. She resolved right there that she'd make the effort to take the time for herself.

Michal Poe

As she sipped her lemon ice, she felt death was far removed from her little circle for now. She couldn't help but think of her mother's favorite old saying, *One Life—Endless Blessings.*

The End